The Memoirs of Eunice Oh

A Life Story of Being My True Self

The Memoirs of Eunice Oh
A Life Story of Being My True Self

1st printing August 21, 2023 ⓒ 2023 by Eunice Oh

Dong-Yeon Press
Address: 2nd FL. #163-3 Worldcup-Ro, Mapo-Ku, Seoul, Korea
Tel: +82-2-335-2630 Fax: +82-2-335-2640
e-mail: yh4321@gmail.com
SNS: instagram.com/dongyeon_press
Publication registration number: 1-1383(June 12, 1992)

ISBN 978-89-6447-927-8 03040

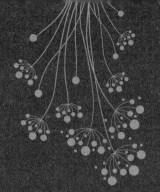

The
Memoirs of
Eunice Oh

A Life Story of Being My True Self

Eunice Oh (오유순)
Trans. by Eugene Oh

Dong
Yeon
Press

Remarks
The Honourable Yonah Martin, Senator

SENATE   SÉNAT
The Honourable Yonah Martin   L'honorable Yonah Martin

CANADA

November 2022

CONGRATULATORY MESSAGE FROM THE HONOURABLE YONAH MARTIN

I am honoured to congratulate Mrs. Eunice Oh on the publication of her memoir, a book inspired by a life well lived.

Ralph Waldo Emerson's writes "...to know that even one life has breathed easier because you have lived...is to have succeeded". By this definition, Eunice Oh has achieved immeasurable success.

As an iconic pioneer of the regional and national Korean Canadian community, she has been a visionary leader and philanthropist willing to give her time and support with graciousness and compassion. As former Chair of the Vancouver Korean Canadian Scholarship Foundation, Chair of the Rose of Sharon Foundation and a willing contributor of various charitable endeavours, she has made great contributions to the wider society and brought hope and light into the lives of many.

As an example, the Korean floor within the New Vista long term care home could not have been built without the generosity and vision of Eunice Oh. Thanks to Eunice Oh's generous donation, Korean elders in care can live their lives with greater comfort and receive culturally-specific care.

Eunice Oh's life story - from pioneering immigrant to community leader, philanthropist and outstanding recipient of the Senate 150 medal in Canada's 150th anniversary year (2017) - is worth telling and reading.

May her book enlighten and inspire all who have the opportunity to come across its pages.

With sincere respect,

The Honourable Yonah Martin
Senator

Senate of Canada Building, Parliament Hill, Ottawa, Ontario K1A 0A4 | martin@sen.parl.gc.ca

My wife is writing her memoirs. I refer to her as my wife, but, as her memoirs make clear, she is that and she is much more than that.

We got married in May 1970 and emigrated from South Korea in January 1971 so that I could continue my studies in Canada. From the beginning of our marriage, she supported me tirelessly as I completed my doctorate in religious studies at McMaster University in Hamilton, Ontario, Canada. She took care of our first son, who was born shortly after we arrived in Canada, and our second son, who was born not long thereafter, all while ensuring that I would be able to focus on my studies, even staying up nights to type up reports and papers I'd completed just before they were due. Back then she was truly a housewife and indeed the queen of housewives.

Whether it was because she wanted to make use of her master's degree in pharmacy, or because she wanted to make the most of her potential, or because she was uncertain about our future after I obtained my PhD, she studied for the Canadian Pharmacist Qualification Exam and received her license to practice in Ontario even while working as a housewife. When we moved to Winnipeg so that I could take a position at the University of Manitoba, she got a Manitoba pharmacist's license. When I moved to the University of Alberta, she obtained her license to practice in

Alberta. And when I moved to the University of Regina, she got a Saskatchewan license.

I'm kidding when I say this, but if there is anything I've done for her, it is giving her the opportunity to live in almost all of Canada in this way. As a professor, I had long summer vacations, so we were able to travel all over North America, east to west, from the Atlantic to the Pacific, and north to south, from Canada all through the United States to Mexico, and, when the North American Academy of Religion met each year, she would travel with me to various locations around North America, which above all else liberated her from her Christian faith.

I received tenure at the University of Regina, and we were a close-knit family of five, with three sons, doing well. Then our oldest went to the University of British Columbia in Vancouver on the Pacific coast, and our second son followed two years later. My wife traveled to Vancouver to visit the kids and called me long distance saying she loved the climate and wanted to move there. And she'd already signed the contract on the purchase of a home.

I happened to be on sabbatical at the time and didn't have to go to school for another year, so we moved to Vancouver in the summer of 1991 and shortly thereafter she got her British Columbia pharmacist's license and opened her own pharmacy. From that point on, she became so active outside of the house, the term "housewife" was no longer a fitting description.

At the beginning of our marriage, I half-jokingly said, "As we go through life, you make all of the small decisions, and I will make only the big ones." So far, however, I feel like I've had very few big decisions to make. The ones I've had to think about are, how can I help people understand religion more deeply, how can I help promote the reunification of North and South Korea, and how can I contribute to achieving world peace? So, every summer vacation, I wrote articles for community newspapers, and I presented lectures about interfaith peace as it relates to furthering reconciliation and cooperation between North and South Korea, because it is said that without interfaith peace there can be no world peace.

In retrospect, however, I feel that, ever since we moved to Vancouver, all those concerns have been taken over by my wife as well. Despite working as a pharmacist and tending to the healthcare needs of her customers, she also finds time to travel to South Korea to attend conferences as a member of the Peaceful Unification Advisory Council, she has made multiple trips to North Korea as a board member of First Steps, an organization that provides soy milk to North Korean children, and she has attended the World Summit of Nobel Peace Laureates, an annual gathering of Nobel Peace Prize winners. Now I jokingly say that as a religious studies major, I feel the only decision I can make is whether to believe there is a heaven in the sky.

Since moving to Vancouver, in addition to doing the work I've listed above, she has grown beyond being just a housewife to become a public figure, variously through her work developing and leading the Vancouver Korean-Canadian Scholarship Foundation, serving as its chair for three years; her leadership role in founding the Rose of Sharon Foundation, where she currently serves as president; and through her donations to New Vista, a Vancouver-area operator of care homes, for the construction of a new building where one floor is dedicated to housing Korean residents.

The details are in her memoirs, so I don't need to repeat them. In any case, I think it's good to have a record of how a woman lived as an immigrant, as a wife, and as a mother of three sons, and how in addition to that she strived to contribute in a meaningful way to her community, and if reading her story inspires somebody to do things similarly worthwhile, I think that would be even better.

Congratulations, honey, on the publication of your memoirs.

Life is God's greatest gift. Even now, when I open my eyes at dawn, I am filled with gratitude for the gift of today. It has been a long, sometimes difficult journey to this point, but my life today is the result of that journey, in the way a pearl is created through hardship. Never have I taken for granted the gift that is my life.

As I begin each morning with meditation, when I think about the tasks before me that day, knowing what I need to do comes naturally and it moves my heart. And there is no greater blessing than being able to do the work. Bringing happiness to my family, my customers, my fellow Canadians, and anybody who crosses my path is a calling that inspires me and brings me joy.

It is important to take care of your health. May my hands and feet follow diligently where my heart wants to go! May my body age more slowly than my mind! Swimming and golf are my favorite activities because they are healthy and fun. I think key to being healthy is daily exercise whatever the weather, proper nutrition, and restful sleep.

Is it said that life is a journey? When looking back at my life in writing this memoir, I see four distinct phases: growing up as a child in my parents' loving care and working hard in school and church; immigrating to Canada with my husband and working as a pharmacist while raising our three sons; moving to Vancouver, opening a dispensary, and building a financial foundation;

and becoming president of the Vancouver Korean-Canadian Scholarship Foundation and working for the community.

I have written this story of my life going back step by step from recent years to when I was young. I hope this process of reflecting on my journey will be an opportunity to see that life is a gift given to everyone. I hope that my story will be interesting and useful to others.

Chapter 1 :

Service

1. Building a Korean nursing home and the Rose of Sharon Foundation

A low-income housing development recently constructed in Burnaby is to be named the Eunice Oh Residence. Initially, I was embarrassed and felt undeserving of such an honor, so I declined. I was not the only one who donated to New Vista's project. Financial contributions came from all over the Korean-Canadian community in the Vancouver area, including the Rose of Sharon Foundation. I was uncomfortable with the idea of having only my name recognized, as it did not reflect the collective efforts of the community.

But Darin Froese, the CEO of New Vista, explained why it was a good idea, and it made an impression on me. He said that society needs positive role models and that this recognition might inspire others to follow my example. Hearing those words made me realize that the recognition could serve as a catalyst for moving others to contribute. If that were to occur and even one person benefits, I would be happy to donate my name.

Vancouver's Korean-Canadian community had recognized the need for a culturally sensitive nursing home for some time, and as a pharmacist who serves many elderly patients in this community, I understood the critical importance of such care. I see many elderly Koreans become extremely anxious when it comes time to move into a nursing facility because the language, the food, and

朝鮮日報

VANCHOSUN MEDIA

버나비에 '오유순 이사장' 이름 딴 레지던스 지어진다

오유순 이사장 뉴비스타에 공립 한인 양로원 건립 위해 100만달러 쾌척

the people are all unfamiliar, making it an unsuitable environment for them. I vividly remember one of my father's friends, Kim Kook-jin, who was told by his doctor that it was time for him to enter a nursing home but refused. Ultimately, he went on a fast and passed away. I cannot forget the shock I felt at the time. This experience reinforced my belief in the necessity of a nursing home for Korean seniors, and I began working with people in the community to find a way to build one.

I traveled all over the Lower Mainland meeting with city officials to advocate for the construction of a Korean nursing home. Through these efforts, I developed close relationships with several officials. I came to know Derek Corrigan, who was the mayor of Burnaby at the time, Maxine Wilson, who was the mayor of Coquitlam, and Richard Stewart, currently the mayor of Coquitlam, particularly well. They were supportive of our community and receptive to our ideas. As there are many immigrant communities in Canada, however, they were unable to allocate all their resources solely to benefit the Korean-Canadian community. Therefore, we would need to find our own way forward.

I approached Darin Froese, CEO of New Vista, a company that constructs and manages residential care homes in the Vancouver area, to propose a partnership for building a nursing facility for Korean seniors. New Vista was experiencing its own financial challenges at the time, so my proposal was accepted. In July 2017, we signed a memorandum of understanding whereby I personally donated $1 million in a lump sum, the Rose of Sharon

Foundation and the Mugunghwa Women's Association agreed to donate $50,000 per year for 10 years, and New Vista committed to dedicating one floor of its new nursing home to provide culturally sensitive care to Korean seniors.

At long last, in October 2020, the new facility was complete, with the entire second floor dedicated to a Korean care home, and Korean seniors began taking residence. The Korean Canadian care floor was contracted for subsidized housing, meaning low-income residents paid only $1,000 of the $7,000 monthly cost, with the remainder covered by the British Columbia government. We arranged for the installation of heated flooring and traditional Korean-style windowpanes, and Korean-speaking staff members were available around the clock. We paid special attention to the menu program,

making sure it was tailored to the residents, and we responded quickly to any feedback. I wanted to ensure the residents were receiving care that made them feel secure and happy and gave them a taste of home in Korea.

It was heartwarming to witness so many elderly Korean-Canadians able to live in comfort here. Although it was a challenging endeavor,

With Jongho Kyun, consul general of the Republic of Korea, and Maria Nam at the New Vista Care Home, 2023.

we came together as a community to make it happen, and the experience was deeply moving for me personally. For those of us who had been trying so hard to build this place, it was a blessing. Don't we all wish we could spend the last years of our lives receiving professional care in a comfortable environment? I am so happy that this long-held dream has been realized, as I would like to spend my final hours here. I will continue to dream and live for the Korean-Canadian community. As long as I'm alive and breathing, I will continue to do my utmost to make that dream a reality.

In 2008, a group of women from the Korean-Canadian community in Vancouver came together to form the Rose of Sharon Foundation and the Mugunghwa Women's Association with the intention of helping those in need and working for the betterment of the Korean-Canadian community. In the first year of our organization, we held a bazaar to raise funds for the creation of a Korean nursing home and we have continued to hold a bazaar every year since. Initially, the bazaar took place in front of HanNam Supermarket in Coquitlam's Koreatown, but it is now

With New Vista CEO Darin Froese, April 2022.

With family at the site of the new Eunice Oh Residence building, August 2022.

With BC MLA Anne Kang (far left), New Vista CEO Darin Froese (fourth from left), and Burnaby city councilor Paul McDonell (second from right) at the New Vista Care Home groundbreaking ceremony, January 26, 2019.

held at New Vista Care Home.

We advertised in newspapers and posted flyers asking for donations of clothing, kitchen utensils, handbags, shoes, and other items from the community, which were sent to Oh Pharmacy. Through the sale of these items, we were able to raise about $3,000 or $4,000 every year, and we also received monetary donations.

At the suggestion of Hwang Seung-il, an attorney, we adopted the name the Rose of Sharon Foundation (Rose of Sharon is the English name of Mugunghwa, the national flower of South Korea) and applied to become a registered charity. This enabled us to issue official donation receipts and thereby attract more donors.

Much of our early efforts revolved around providing relief funding to places affected by natural disasters worldwide. In 2010, our

With members of the Rose of Sharon Women's Association at our annual bazaar, 2022. Front row from left: Woo Ae-kyung, Cho Chun-soon, Lee Yeon-sim, Kim Kyung-ja, Anna Baek, Kim In-soon, Lee Jung-im, Kim Kyung-ae, Oh Yoo-soon. Back row from left: Kate Kim, Choi Eun-mi, Laula Kim, Cha Min-joon.

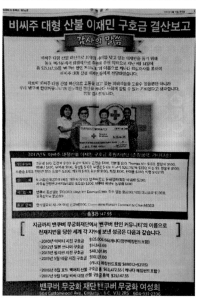

foundation collected donations from Korean businesses, churches, organizations, and individuals and together with matching funds from the Canadian government was able to send $120,006.66 to Haiti for earthquake relief. In 2012, after the Japan tsunami, we held a multicultural walk to raise money. The event was a success, despite the rainy weather, with participation from community members all around the Vancouver area. Because of Japan's remarks made around that time regarding Dokdo, however, we were able to deliver just $14,843.69. Building on those early efforts, we have been able to raise $40,301.85 to help earthquake victims in the Philippines in 2013, $90,127.00 to support relief efforts following the May 2015

At a Korean food festival in 2012.

With early members of the Rose of Sharon Foundation, including Senator Yonah Martin, Kim Kyung-ae, Kim Kyung-ja, Kim In-soon, Bae Eun-young, Anna Paik, Woo Ae-kyung, and Jin Young-ran at the Korean-Canadian Care Home Fundraising Bazaar in 2017.

With Kim In-soon, Kim Kyung-ja, Jin Young-ran, Woo Ae-kyung, Kim Kyung-ae, Bae Eun-young, and others at a Mugunghwa Women's Association bazaar in 2019.

earthquake in Nepal, $63,472.55 for disaster relief after the August 2016 Fort McMurray wildfire, $5,000 for disaster aid after the May 2016 earthquake in Ecuador, and $25,147.55 to aid recovery efforts following the 2017 BC wildfires. All of these donations were made on behalf of the Korean-Canadian community of Vancouver, Canada.

The original members of the Rose of Sharon Foundation and Women's Association who first gathered in 2008 continue to work diligently for the community, and many new members have joined the organization over the years. We have developed a strong camaraderie as a result of working together, which provides motivation for the organization. Even now, a shelf at Oh Pharmacy is reserved for Rose of Sharon Foundation bazaar donations. While we had to take a break due to the coronavirus, we were able to restart the bazaar in 2022, raising over $4,000.

2. Vancouver Korean Association

I think the president of the Vancouver Korean Association should of course be sensitive to the needs of the members of the Korean-Canadian community. In addition to listening to the individual voices, however, he or she should also consider the desirable role of the Korean immigrant community as a whole in Canada and find ways to fulfill that role together. Therefore, as president of the Vancouver Korean Association, I have tried to make the organization into a center where Koreans living in Vancouver area can come together.

However, this hasn't been without its challenges. To reduce expenses, I took over the duties of the paid office manager myself, leaving me with not enough hours in the day. The Korean community center was also located in a high-crime neighborhood, and the security alarm would often go off in the middle of the night. I would have to wake my sleeping husband, and we would make the one-hour drive from Coquitlam to the community center. It was scary to go to East Hastings in the dark.

Despite these challenges, there are many happy memories from around that time. One that stands out is dressing in a hanbok and waving the Korean flag at the airport to welcome Kim Yuna and the other Korean athletes arriving for the Vancouver Olympics. Also, there was the time we invited marathoner Lee Bong-ju to headline a 10K run in Burnaby, and we were able to have the singers Yoon

Hyung-joo and Kim Se-hwan perform at an event we held to raise funds for a new Korean community center. Other events included a festival to celebrate Daeboreum and a Korean expo.

I became president of the Vancouver Korean Association in 2009, shortly before the Vancouver Winter Olympics took place, in February 2010, so one of my first efforts as president was to bring our community together to show our support for the Korean athletes who were competing. We broadcast the events at Korea Plaza in front of HanNam Supermarket, where we could watch together and cheer on our athletes. South Korea's national team, which included Kim Yuna, Lee Sang-hwa, and Lee Seung-hoon, had a very successful performance at the Vancouver games. I was fortunate enough to be able to be in attendance to cheer them on. The excitement was indescribable!

Seeing Kim Yuna draped in the Korean national flag brought tears to my eyes. I felt so proud of her, but also I thought about the long road, all the way from childhood, it must have been to get to this point, and I thought about the happiness of this achievement, all the hard work, the joy of winning gold. I was flooded with all kinds of emotions. Probably all Koreans experienced something similar in this moment. So, we wanted to support not just Kim Yuna but also all of the Korean competitors.

In preparation for the games, we wanted to acquire a large stock of Korean flags in various sizes to hand out. We wanted to show our support to the Korean athletes by displaying them everywhere we could and waving them at their competitions. We passed them out to people in the stands, regardless of whether they were Korean, and we saw a great number in the crowds. This received a good amount of media coverage, and I gave many interviews as president of the organization responsible for providing many of the flags. Although I missed seeing the interviews when they aired, my friends in Korea contacted me to say they'd seen me on TV.

The actual task of getting so many Korean flags took much more effort than I expected. For one thing, it was difficult to find the flags in Canada, so I would have to travel to Korea to get them, and it took a lot of time and money to find suppliers there, order the quantities that we wanted, and transport the flags back to Canada. I bought every size and type of flag I could find and came back with two gigantic rolling suitcases filled with them, and it was such a relief! The work did not seem arduous, though, because I was happy to be doing something for my motherland.

After competitions, we took our flags and marched through the streets of downtown. It was the Olympics, Kim Yuna had won a gold medal, there was no one to say anything, so I joyfully waved the flag to my heart's content along with the other Koreans living in Canada. From the time the national team arrived in Canada to when the athletes returned to Korea, we accompanied them all around waving the flag. In particular, Kim Sung-hwan, who was in charge of general affairs at the time, was a man with great energy who encouraged all of us in the Korean immigrant community to go out and wave our flags.

Following the Winter Olympics were the Winter Paralympic

Games and to welcome the Korean athletes to our community center we arranged for the installation of wheelchair-friendly facilities in the building and served a catered meal, and later we followed them to Whistler to cheer them on in their events. I did the best I could to treat them.

The surprising thing was that while we thought we were doing

this for the sake of the athletes, in reality, we were also benefiting, coming together as a community and becoming further united. I think it was a good opportunity to gather, expand our network, and strengthen existing relationships.

On September 4, 2010, we hosted a 10K run with Olympic silver medalist marathon runner Lee Bong-ju. We had heard from the Korean consulate that he was visiting Toronto, so we got in contact to ask whether he would be interested in making a stop in Vancouver while in Canada. The moment we received word that he was, we began organizing a 10K run, calling it Autumn Family Health Walk with Lee Bong-ju. With an estimated 400 people expected to participate, there would be many logistical issues to take care of, but we proceeded with the mindset that by working together there was nothing we couldn't do.

When I look back on this event, what comes to mind are all the unexpected twists and turns. Perhaps the biggest was receiving word that Mr. Lee could not come on the scheduled date. All of the preparation we'd made up to that point, from booking the venue to securing the support of the mayor of Burnaby, hiring the vendors, and scheduling volunteers, was based on the assumption that the event would

take place on that particular date. The news of Mr. Lee's absence threatened to derail our plans completely. I was driving when I received the news, and I remember I had to pull over into a nearby alley, stopping the car so that I could cry and make some urgent phone calls. Fortunately, the problem was ultimately resolved, but even now when I drive by that alley where I stopped to make those phone calls the memory of that day comes flooding back to me and my face gets heated.

Another challenge we faced was locating and securing a park that could accommodate 400 people for a 10K run and a picnic. The process involved dealing with legal and administrative matters, getting permits, arranging for police details, managing trash disposal, and obtaining insurance coverage, none of which was straightforward. With so many things requiring my attention, the task seemed overwhelming at times, and needless to say I had to learn a lot, but in the end, we were able to get it done.

A third difficulty was rain on the day of the event. The other issues were ones I could address through my own efforts, but weather was really beyond my control. People were coming to me for guidance, how were we to do this? It appeared we would have to cancel the event. After a moment of uncertainty, I thought about all the work that had gone into making this event happen, and I made the decision to push ahead with our plans. We set up canopies and awnings that would provide shelter from the rain. I was so pleased and happy to see our organization able to work so quickly to respond to this latest challenge.

Fortunately, the rain stopped shortly thereafter, and the event was able to continue without further complication. It was a spectacular sight: 400 Koreans running, walking, pushing strollers, together. The newly appointed Korean consul general in Vancouver, Choi Yeon-ho, attended the event that day. An avid athlete, he completed the 10 km run, while others ran as much as they could and then relaxed and enjoyed the day in the park.

It was no easy feat to gather such a large group in one place, but coming together with one heart, while respecting each another's pace, held great meaning for me. Seeing all the happy faces made all the hard work worthwhile. When I think back on the time we spent preparing food for 400 people and creating event mementos for Lee Bong-ju and the participants, it is with a sense of satisfaction. I am especially grateful to the members of the Vancouver Korean Association. The event would not have been possible without these kind individuals who worked so tirelessly at my side despite the hardships they had to endure.

On April 24, 2010, we hosted a concert featuring Yoon Hyung-joo and Kim Se-hwan at Pacific Academy to raise funds for the construction of a new community center. The existing Korean community center was in poor condition, and I remember running in all directions around that time to raise money through various means, including concert proceeds and sponsorships, with the goal of building a new and improved one.

The auditorium at Pacific Academy has a seating capacity of approximately 1,600 people. Kim Sung-hwan, secretary of the

Vancouver Korean Association, was instrumental in selling that many tickets. A talented singer and musician himself, he would busk in front of HanNam Supermarket every weekend, singing songs by Kim Se-Hwan and Yoon Hyung-joo. We would stand nearby, holding up publicity posters and sell tickets to anyone passing by.

Thanks to these efforts, the tickets sold well, the audience would fill the seats, and it appeared the show would go on without a hitch, but there was something I hadn't foreseen: the auditorium had poor acoustics. This information blindsided me. I didn't know anything about sound systems, so when on the day of the concert the singers pointed out the poor quality, I had no idea what to do. It felt like a nightmare.

We could have proceeded anyway, but I wanted to do it right,

not settle for anything less than that, so I ran to the sound technician for help. Fortunately, the issues were taken care of just in time, but once things were going smoothly and I was watching the concert begin, I realized my throat was burning. The water I drank at that time was so cool. Thanks to this experience, I try to listen to everybody's input whatever it is we're doing. I have found that taking the step to consider all perspectives increases the chance of success.

The concert generated approximately $130,000 in proceeds from ticket sales and sponsorships from businesses, alumni associations, and media. The funds were deposited in the Rose of Sharon Foundation's account, bringing the total amount earmarked for the new community center to around $160,000 after my personal contribution. I eagerly anticipate the day when we can break ground on its construction and witness the fruits of our labor. It has been a long process, but I am grateful for having been able to be a part of it. When I assumed the presidency of the Vancouver Korean Association, the organization was $145,682.22 in debt. Our efforts to turn things around have yielded significant improvements, and we are now seeing the results.

On January 15, 2010, in celebration of the Korean holiday Daeboreum, we followed tradition and paraded through the streets, stopping at various businesses, both Korean-owned and not, to wish them good luck for the coming year and distribute gifts. As we made our way from HanNam Supermarket on North Road in Coquitlam and headed north, we were accompanied

by the vibrant sounds of Hanchanghyun Samulnori, a Korean percussion ensemble. It was a day filled with warmth and celebration as we visited the businesses in our community and shared in the festive spirit of the occasion.

With so many of us participating, everyone wearing colorful hanboks and dancing, we attracted a lot of attention and much curiosity. It was a nice opportunity to introduce Korean culture and talk about our traditions to our fellow Canadians. In Canada, there is the custom of sending New Year's greetings and this was similar to that.

The mayors of Coquitlam and Burnaby were very supportive of our community, joining us for the parade wearing the hanboks we had given them as gifts. I learned how to play the percussion instruments used for samulnori. So that was one more thing to add to the long list of things I learned while president of the Vancouver Korean Association.

On October 28, 2010, the Vancouver Korean Association held a blood drive. Our campaign started with the hope of increasing the number of Koreans who donate blood and was the idea of Kim Sung-eun, who had been volunteering in other blood drives before joining our organization. We held pre-registration events in front of H Mart and HanNam Supermarket, and members of the Vancouver Korean Association signed up to give blood.

Ms. Kim had been working on blood drives with Canadian Blood Services for two years, having been moved to volunteer after the experience of a family member who received a blood transfusion. That is what it means to help one another! By practicing gratitude for the grace we have received and doing so through service, we can create a virtuous cycle of grace and kindness in our society!

한인회 '사랑의 헌혈 캠페인'

10월28일 오후 1시부터, 사전 등록 받아

밴쿠버한인회에서는 '사랑의 헌혈 캠페인'을 오는 10월 28일(목) 오후 1시부터 저녁 8시까지 빌 코프랜드 스포츠 콤플렉스(Bill Copeland Sports Complex)에서 실시한다. 헌혈을 위한 사전 등록은 10월 16일(토)과 17일(일), 그리고 23일(토)과 24일(일) 각각 오후 2시부터 5시까지 한아름마켓과 한남마켓 앞에서 받는다.

'사랑의 헌혈 캠페인'은 캐나다헌혈협회(Canada Blood Service)에서 꾸준히 봉사활동을 해오고 있는 김성은 씨가 독자적으로 벌여오던 것을 올해부터는 한인회 차원에서 함께 하게 됐다.

김성은 씨는 "한인들이 많이 참여해서 사랑의 헌혈에 함께 할 수 있으면 하는 바람에서 한인회에 함께 캠페인을 벌이고 있다"면서 "현재 헌혈협회에 '코리안 커뮤니티' 라는 이름으로등록이 되어 있어 헌혈하는 한인들의 수가 커뮤니티 안에 추가되어 이것이 연말에 합산된다"고 말했다.

작년의 경우 많은 한인들이 참여해 협회로부터 '코리안 커뮤니티' 가 표창장을 받기도 했다.

김씨는 "나 한 사람이 참여하는 것이 한인사회의 캐나다 사회 기여를 상징하는 것" 이라며 관심을 촉구했다.

김성은 씨는 가족중의 한 사람이 많은 피가 요구되는 상황을 겪으면서 헌혈의 중요성을 깨닫게 되었다. 그 후 캐나다헌혈협회의 자원봉사자로 꾸준히 활동해오면서 2년 전부터 독자적으로 헌혈 캠페인을 벌여왔다.

헌혈 장소: Bill Copeland Sports Complex(주소: 3676 Kensington Ave., Burnaby)

문의: 한인회(604-255-3739), 웹사이트 www.vancouverkoreans.ca, 김성은(604-733-5656)

> **"한국일보가 10월6일부터 매주 '수·금·토'에 발행합니다."**
> "더욱 신속하고 알찬 정보로 독자들께 기쁨과 만족을 드리겠습니다"

I believe that the Vancouver Korean Association can be where like-minded people can come together to make a positive impact through their collective efforts.

The success of our blood drive demonstrated what can be accomplished when we join forces. It was also heartwarming to see so many Koreans step up to give blood for their neighbors in need. I was proud of our community, which had come together to do good for the benefit of society.

On May 12, 2012, we held a Korean business expo. We saw a need among new immigrants for help navigating their way as they settled into their lives in Canada, so we invited experts to give talks, provide consultations, and deliver seminars gratis. Topics ranged across subjects such as how to reach out to the Korean consulate general, mortgages, retirement planning, personal finance, pensions, job hunting, healthcare, estate planning, English-language education, early childhood education, family counseling, computer and IT training, immigration law, and the educational system in Canada.

The expo occupied almost an entire medical office building, with signage outside each room guiding attendees to where they could find the information they were seeking. Life as a new immigrant is hugely challenging, so the fact that our organization could help people find solutions and improve their quality of life was greatly gratifying to me.

So that is why I was glad to provide the venue for this event for free. BC government agencies had expressed interest in leasing the property for office space, but I wanted to keep the space available for Korean association events. Even though this meant giving up about $300,000 a year in rental income, it was a hundred times more rewarding to have my building be used for something more valuable than that. Also around that time, my mother who had been living with me passed away unexpectedly. The event was scheduled to take place only a week after her funeral. I was encouraged to cancel the expo, but I didn't, because its value was so precious to me. Serving the Korean

community is something I am deeply involved in and pour all my passion into.

With Kim Doo-yeol, Lee Ken-Beck, and Korean consul general Choi Yeon-ho after receiving a presidential award (JoongAng Ilbo, November 5, 2010).

With Representative Sohn Hak-kyu of the Korean Democratic Party at the 2011 World President's Congress Celebration Dinner.

3. Ewha Womans University Alumnae Association of North America and supporting Korean-Canadian politicians

In 2012, I was elected president of the Ewha Womans University Alumnae Association of North America, and in October of that year, was tasked with organizing a reunion in Vancouver hosting 300 attendees including the presidents of the North American chapters, university alumnae, and the university president. They would visit for three nights and four days, and we planned an itinerary that included a tour of the city, a talent show, and other social events.

Holding such a large-scale event of course presented many challenges, but we were able to pull it off with the help of many alumnae volunteering their services. One thing we had to do was create a yearbook to send to university alumnae located all over the world, and in this undertaking, I was very grateful to be able

With Ewha Womans University President Kim Sun-wook.

to rely on Bae Eun-young, a fellow alumna and the operator of a print shop. Being able to reach out to alumnae all over the world and help each other, I could see that we truly were an international community, and it made my experience a rewarding one.

The event was at the Hilton Hotel, and along with Ewha University president Kim Sun-wook, we went on a tour to Lynn Valley, and the service was first class. At the talent show, the alumnae from Vancouver danced to Gangnam Style, which at the time was at the height of its popularity, and the contingent from San Francisco performed a play that one of them had written, making for a very entertaining show. On the final night, we sang the national anthem and the school song by candlelight, and it was a touching moment that brought tears to the eyes of everybody in attendance.

After such a meaningful gathering, we had a deepened affection for one another, and I think we all returned to our respective homes knowing we were part of a community that transcended borders and we could rely on each other if we were to ever need help in our immigrant lives.

The following is an essay written by Ewha Womans

University Alumnae Association of North America Vancouver chapter president and Can-Kor publishing company president Sophia Bae, who has been of invaluable assistance to me for over 30 years with her unwavering dedication and support. It appeared in the 2012 Yearbook of the Ewha Womans University North America Alumnae Association.

Waiting for Godot

By Sophia Bae
Ewha Womans University, Department of Christian Studies, 1990
Ewha Womans University Alumnae Association of North America Vancouver chapter president

One day after I turned 40, thoughts of Samuel Beckett's work Waiting for Godot kept popping into my head. So, I began paging through the dusty copy I had on my desk.

At the end of the long wait, Godot does not appear.

The sadness burns into my heart, yet Godot does not appear.

Then one day there appeared before me a person like Godot.

That person was Ewha Womans University alumna Kang Yoo-Soon (Eunice Yoo-Soon Oh).

I seem to remember it was in 2002. A staff member from the Vancouver Korean-Canadian Scholarship Foundation came to my design and printing company with an urgent print order. At the time, Ms. Kang had recently taken over as chair of the foundation, which back then was still a small organization. While working on the print job, I came to know the scholarship foundation and as it grew I watched from the sidelines.

When I started my business, there were very few companies that provided both graphic design and printing services, so whenever an organization in the Korean community in Vancouver had a need for promotional or event-related material my company would often be the one to create it. In this way, I was able to see how Korean organizations in Vancouver operated and specifically the way they prepared for their annual events.

Since Ms. Kang became chair of the scholarship foundation, the foundation's annual awards ceremony has become a major event in Vancouver's Korean-Canadian community. Of course, the revolutionary change that the organization underwent to achieve this success and its remarkable growth were largely the results of Ms. Kang's efforts. One day, I happened to run into Ms. Kang at a law office, and during our conversation I offhandedly suggested there should be a women's association in the Korean community, and soon after, she was establishing the nonprofit organization that would become the Rose of Sharon Foundation.

It is quite scary how quickly Ms. Kang turns thoughts into actions and in this characteristic I feel she is unmatched. After struggling for some time to realize her vision of building a

Korean nursing home and a Korean community center with the Rose of Sharon Foundation, she became president of the Vancouver Korean Association, which gave her greater authority. When I moved to Vancouver in 1993, I was appalled and upset to see the shabby state of the Korean community center. Were Korean Vancouverites so poor that they would neglect their community center like this? Where were all the Christians?

I think the work Waiting for Godot suddenly came to mind as I watched the Korean community center fall further and further into decline with the passing years.

The Vancouver Korean Association was drowning in debt, and the center was in dire need of repair, and the organization was riddled with problems. The decrepit building, the sniping among the members, the disorganization -- it was a life of absurdity and despair. It was not unlike the setting described by Samuel Beckett in Waiting for Godot.

I was amazed by Ms. Kang's enthusiasm as she dove into that environment of despair and immediately I thought of the Godot whom I had been waiting for.

The situation at the Vancouver Korean Association reminded me of a story I'd once heard. The story goes that a doctor was performing surgery to remove a cancerous tumor from a patient's stomach but found that the cancer had spread so much that all he could do was sew the patient back together. If I were in Ms. Kang's place, I would probably have left the association as soon as I realized the state it was in, like the doctor leaving the operating room.

But for some reason Ms. Kang wanted to be president of the association. If I had her wealth, I would just spend the rest of my years traveling and enjoying my life. But when I saw her continue to persevere despite all the criticism, I was reminded of pioneers such as Ewha Womans University presidents Kim Hwal-lan, Kim Ok-gil, Chang Sang, and Shin In-ryung, and Professor Park Soon-kyung, all of whom were pillars of modernization and were responsible for so much progress for Korean women.

If you know the history of the Korean community in Vancouver, you would see that it is time for the construction of a proper community center, but nobody is willing to come forward to take on the work.

Many people have been reluctant to come forward because they are too modest, but if there is a real need for action and nobody is responding to the call, that is not modesty but instead inaction and neglect. There are many people in the Korean community who have the necessary skills and leadership qualities, and there are many people who have succeeded in business and have great financial resources, but they seem reluctant to get involved in matters that serve their community.

Some people see the Vancouver Korean Association and say, "If you're an egret, don't go where the crows are playing." You might agree with the sentiment, but how long will we continue to criticize the organization that represents our community in

Canada as it slides further into decline?

The Japanese, with its history of inflicting sorrow and humiliation on the Korean people, have built the Nikkei National Museum and Cultural Center, which honors and preserves their heritage, and a nursing home in Burnaby, while the Chinese have created a powerful organization called SUCCESS., which has dozens of branches all over the Metro Vancouver area. SUCCESS has an annual operating budget of $36 million, 80% of which comes from the Canadian government. The money is funneled back into the Chinese community, so their power continues to snowball.

How long will we, the Korean community in Vancouver, continue to criticize, doubt, and look the other way? In the Bible, God said he would not destroy Sodom and Gomorrah if there were just 10 righteous people, but not even 10 could be found in these cities and they were destroyed. I find it hard to believe there were no egrets in those cities. On the contrary, I think there were more egrets than crows. But God did not count them as righteous and chose to punish them along with the wicked.

If a person remains silent in a corrupt society, that person becomes a sympathizer. We cannot call that person an egret. If the person is an intellect, we cannot respect his or her intelligence. If that person is of means, we cannot place any authority on that wealth. Such a person would be nothing more than a shell wearing intelligence as an accessory and a greedy

rich person like Scrooge in A Christmas Carol. We cannot recognize and do not respect their value.

From her time serving as chair of the Vancouver Korean-Canadian Scholarship Foundation to founding the Mugunghwa Foundation to becoming president of the Vancouver Korean Association, Ms. Kang has faced criticism and negative public opinion for all sorts of things. Rather than those who sit and criticize without doing anything themselves, however, it is Ms. Kang who strives to do the work despite the challenges and devotes herself to a worthy cause, and ultimately, she is the pioneer and the critics are not.

Being human means being imperfect. Everybody has

weaknesses and makes errors, and that is only natural. There are certainly enough weaknesses, limitations, and errors in my own thinking. But even if flawed, anybody who dedicates his or her time and resources in service of the community should be met with encouragement and respect, not criticism, and indeed we should help to fill in the deficiencies and make up for the limitations. Wouldn't that be the right thing to do?

Lastly, here is an amazing deed that will go down in history. Ms. Kang donated all the condolence money she received at her father's funeral to the Vancouver Korean-Canadian Scholarship Foundation. She also donated all the money she received at her mother's funeral to the v for a new community center. And most recently she donated a million dollars for the construction of a Korean nursing facility.

All of my respect, admiration, and kudos go to Ms. Kang for being a role model for all of us to follow.

In order for the growing Korean community to have a voice, it seems necessary that we have more Korean-Canadians become active in Canadian politics. That is why since the 1990s I have been working to identify and support individuals who could represent us in the political arena. Among my many initiatives in this regard, I think recommending Yonah Martin for her seat in the Senate of Canada is one of the most significant.

When Stephen Harper was prime minister, Tenzin Khangsar, an aide from his office whose wife was Korean, contacted me to ask whether I would be interested in running for office in the upcoming election. I expressed some reservations about running myself but suggested that Yonah Martin would make a great

With BC minister of state for multiculturalism Harry Bloy (far left).

With Canadian prime minister Stephen Harper.

With Canadian prime minister Stephen Harper.

With Canadian prime minister Stephen Harper, Senator Yonah Martin, members of Parliament, and Korean consul general Choi Yeon-ho.

candidate. At the time, Senator Martin was working as an English teacher at Banting Middle School and had impressed me as a good person of strong will and integrity. She was also active in the community as a member of the United Church. After she won the Conservative nomination for the federal election, we campaigned hard together, knocking on doors and engaging with voters. Unfortunately, she lost by a narrow margin.

Not long after the election, Prime Minister Harper remembered a promise he'd made to me and appointed Yonah Martin to serve in the Senate of Canada. When I first recommended her, I had told him that I would recommend a Canadian of Korean descent and he could count on the Korean community for its support. I am grateful to the prime minister for keeping that promise, and

In Burnaby's Central Park for a wreath-laying ceremony on Korean War Veterans Day, 2012.

I am proud of Senator Martin for doing her job as a senator with wisdom and diligence.

Senator Martin has been working assiduously for the Korean community in Canada and is a source of pride for all Korean-Canadians. She is now well known in South Korea as well and often travels there as part of efforts to strengthen the relationship between the two countries. Her notable achievements include the enactment of a bill to make July 27 Korean War Veterans Day and organizing an opportunity for Canadians who had fought in the Korean War to visit the Imjin River in South Korea.

Thanks to Senator Martin, I personally have had many opportunities to travel to Ottawa and attend many government events as an invited guest. One highlight was attending a ceremony to receive a Senate 150th Anniversary Medal, awarded to individuals in recognition of their service to the community. It was an overwhelming honor to be acknowledged among the other recipients, and it also gave me an opportunity to reflect on our work up to that point. It also motivated me to work even harder on the tasks

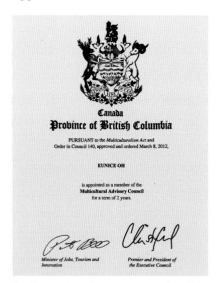

Certificate of appointment as a member of the Multicultural Advisory Council from the Ministry of Jobs, Tourism and Innovation, March 8, 2012.

한인 7명, 캐나다 상원 150주년 메달 수상

오타와서 캐나다 상원 의회 출범 150주년 기념 행사 개최

지난 29일 오타와에서 캐나다 상원 의회 출범 150주년 기념 행사가 열렸다. 이 자리에서 13명의 BC주 주민에게 '상원 150주년 메달'이 수여됐다.

이번 수상자 명단에는 박은숙씨 오름한글문화학교 교장, 서병길 불가리아 명예 영사, 오유

순(무궁화재단 이사장), 우여정(요리 전문가), 이인순(사단법인 벤쿠버 이성회 회장), 이우석(6.25참전 유공자회 회장), 정상이(明두바시 운선교회합창단 지휘자) 등 총 7명의 한인이 영광의 이름을 올렸다.

이외 자선사업가 '단 챔맨(Don Chapman), 명예 대령 하우 리

(Hon. Howe Lee), 다이아몬드 주빌리 메달 수상자 에이미 선드버그(Mrs. Amy Sundberg), 비첼 청소년 전문가 패트릭 토마스(Dr. Patrick Thomas), 섹세스 재단 의양 실여오(Mr. Sing Yeo) 그리고 BC주 한국전쟁기념연합 환전용사 프랭크 스미스(Mr. Frank Smyth) 등이

메달을 수상했다.

캐나다 상원 야당 부대표인 연아 마틴 상원 의원은 상원 의장 조지 퓨리가 주최하는 메달 수여식에 참석해 메달을 수여했다. '상원 150주년 메달'은 캐나다를 보다 살기 위해 봉사한 이름없는 영웅들의 헌신과 공로를 인정하고 표창하기 위해 만들어졌다.

연아 마틴 상원 의원은 "캐나다와 세계를 더 좋은 곳으로 만들기 위해 노력하는 모든 수상자들의 의지와 헌신에 박수를 보낸다"고 전했다.

'상원 150주년 메달' 수상자들은 캐나다 전역에서 보여 가족, 친구, 동료 수상자들이 지켜보는 가운데 메달을 수여했다. 메달 수여식 후 에는 연아 마틴 의원이 주최한 환영 리셉션이 국회의사당에서 열렸다.

또한 수개 캐나다대한민국대사의 신영호 대사가 주최한 만찬 행사도 열렸다. 한편, 정성자 박사와 프랭크 스미스 씨는 12월 중 BC주에서 가족, 친지들과 함께 메달 수여식을 가질 예정이라고 밝혔다.

정봉오 기자

QUEEN ELIZABETH II
DIAMOND JUBILEE MEDAL

MÉDAILLE DU JUBILÉ DE DIAMANT
DE LA REINE ELIZABETH II

Yoo-soon Oh

By Command of Her Majesty The Queen,
the Diamond Jubilee Medal is presented to you
in commemoration of the sixtieth anniversary
of Her Majesty's Accession to the Throne
and in recognition of your contributions to Canada.

Par ordre de Sa Majesté la Reine,
la Médaille du jubilé de diamant vous est présentée
en commémoration du soixantième anniversaire
de l'accession de Sa Majesté au Trône et en reconnaissance
de votre contribution au service du Canada.

Governor General of Canada   Gouverneur général du Canada

1952 - 2012

Certificate conferring the Queen Elizabeth II Diamond Jubilee Medal.

Certificate conferring the Senate 150th Anniversary Medal.

With fellow recipients of the Queen Elizabeth II Diamond Jubilee Medal, 2013.

Eunice OH

Coquitlam, B.C.

Eunice Oh is a tireless community leader. She is the long-standing chair of the Vancouver Korean Canadian Scholarship Foundation, which has awarded nearly $1 million in scholarships to post-secondary students since 1999. She is also the founding chair of the Rose of Sharon Foundation which provides relief funding for places devastated by natural disasters in Canada and the world. Also a generous philanthropist, she recently donated $1 million to New Vista Society for the creation of a new long-term care centre in Burnaby, B.C.

Coquitlam, C.-B.

Eunice Oh est une leader communautaire infatigable. Elle préside depuis longtemps la *Vancouver Korean Canadian Scholarship Foundation*, une organisation qui a remis près d'un million de dollars en bourses d'études à des étudiants de niveau postsecondaire depuis 1999. De plus, elle est la présidente fondatrice de la *Rose of Sharon Foundation*, qui fournit de l'aide financière à des endroits qui ont été dévastés par des catastrophes naturelles au Canada et ailleurs dans le monde. Mécène généreuse, elle a récemment donné un million de dollars à l'organisation *New Vista Society* pour la création d'un établissement de soins de longue durée à Burnaby, en Colombie-Britannique.

Citation for the awarding of the Diamond Jubilee Medal.

In Ottawa to celebrate Canada's 150th Anniversary.

that still lay ahead for the Korean community.

I was first introduced to Shin Jae-kyung while serving as president of the Vancouver Korean Association. It was during a meeting in Burnaby with the city's mayor, Derek Corrigan, who had invited me and Korean consul general Choi Yeon-ho to meet her. She was then a faculty member at BCIT, had good relationships with important Canadian figures, and held political aspirations. She would later become a frequent visitor to my

With Canadian prime minister Justin Trudeau.

pharmacy, where we would discuss topics such as meditation and fasting, which were both great interests of mine.

As the meeting went on, I became aware that Dr. Shin was considering a run for a seat on the British Columbia Legislative Assembly. I was thrilled at the prospect of having a Korean-Canadian MLA and jumped in to offer my support. After she secured the nomination, I organized a Korean community event that raised $60,000 for the campaign. I wrote articles for community newspapers to encourage voter turnout, knocked on doors in the neighborhood, and did everything I could to support her election.

When Baek Kwang-yeol ran for political office during the 1990s, he ran as a Liberal. Senator Yonah Martin is a member of the Conservative Party, and Shin Jae-kyung was running as an NDP candidate. So, I have faced criticism from the Korean community for being so enthusiastic about supporting all of these candidates regardless of party. But it is important to me that the Korean community be represented politically, so I would respond, "I don't care which party. The important thing is that there are Korean-Canadians engaged in politics, whether it's as a Conservative, Liberal, or NDP. I don't support a party. I support Koreans."

It was a joyous occasion when Dr. Shin won the election. She would be a voice for Koreans in Canada, and I knew I had made

With BC MLA Shin Jae-kyung (far left).

a good decision in supporting her. I have had the opportunity to travel to Victoria at her invitation and visit the Parliament Buildings as her guest. While touring the grounds or attending an event, I felt like I was watching a younger sister who made it big. She has all of my support in her endeavors to help the Korean community.

I am also delighted to have supported two other successful campaigns: Steve Kim for Coquitlam City Council and Park Ga-young for a position on Port Moody's Board of Education. It was gratifying to give my support, whether it was through assisting them financially, distributing flyers, approaching individual citizens one by one to ask for their vote, or even providing food for the campaign workers. When they won, we all hugged and shared in the joy of the moment. Even after they were voted into office, they continued to serve their community with dedication, which was rewarded with re-election.

Councilor Steve Kim has continued to do good things for Coquitlam and for the Korean community. He was a longtime chair of the C3 Korean Canadian Society, a nonprofit whose programs include a Korean cultural day, a Camp Korea for children of Korean heritage, and an annual leadership conference for Korean youth. One of C3's cofounders was Yonah Martin, and Steve Kim stepped in as her successor to continue the work of the organization.

Coquitlam mayor Richard Stewart, as well as his predecessor, Maxine Wilson, have been very supportive of the Korean community. I met with them frequently over the many years I spent trying to build a nursing home, and they were always willing to help us and in particular were receptive to the idea of entering a sister-city agreement with Paju, South Korea. Burnaby mayor Derek Corrigan has also been a friend to the Korean community, and played an important role when Burnaby entered a sister-city relationship with Hwaseong, South Korea. All of these mayors have at one time or another attended Korean community events as distinguished guests, coming together despite whatever political differences they may have, to express their support.

It is with great satisfaction that I see the people to whom I gave my wholehearted support achieve great heights in Canadian politics and become leaders whom we can all be proud to call our own. I think they can continue to count on our support.

The following is an essay written by the vice president of the

Vancouver chapter of the Peaceful Unification Advisory Council (PUAC), Kim Kyeong-ae, who has been my right-hand woman with her skill and dedication for the past 20 years.

Thinking of Mrs. Oh

By Kim Kyung-ae

Mugunghwa chair Oh Yoo-soon is my mentor and my closest friend. When I look back to when we began our work together, I am grateful for all of the time we've had together sharing our lives and so many moments of laughter.

Mrs. Oh is, in a word, a wonderful woman. When she has put her mind to something, she is doing it before you know it, and that kind of leadership attracts people and draws them in, whatever the initiative. Her drive and energy, however, also means she tends to overextend herself. She often tackles a task on her own when really it should take a dozen people. Looking on from her side, I see that she must divide her time among a great workload and then she has to divide it further for more work. I must remind her to find time for sleep. Thank you for always spreading positive energy.

Always a steady presence, Mrs. Oh is somebody I admire and wish to emulate. She has said she wants to help create a space for Korean-Canadians in Vancouver and has been going along step by step towards this goal ever since I met her. Despite the many sidelong glances and setbacks, she has resolutely maintained her vision for a community center and a long-term care facility where low-income Korean seniors can live out their remaining years in comfort. Now, here's to your dream, the Korean center! In addition, I wish I had her ability to stay cool whatever she's facing.

Lastly, I really admire Mrs. Oh as a person who gives so much. When she was in charge of fundraising, it was easy to raise funds. We would be seeking donations for disaster relief in Haiti, the Philippines, or some other country, such as Canada following the wildfires, and Mrs. Oh would be the first to make a large financial contribution, setting an example for others to follow, and there was inevitably a positive response. She has also bought a lot of food, not just meals for me but also to feed everyone around us. For example, when she was leading the Vancouver Korean Association, she was quick to open her wallet at board meetings to treat the members. When giving to others, she is generous and has heart. She is, however, a little stingy when it comes to treating herself. She doesn't buy clothes very often. When she is wearing something pretty and I ask her where she got it, she tells me it's something she wore back in the day. At least she has a fair face, so it looks good enough to wear nowadays. And she never throws away food. When she thinks of starving people, she can't throw food away. So, she eats everything in her bowl. Our chair Oh Yoo-soon, who has a caring heart for each and every one of these small things, I will always cheer for you as a friend and comrade and want to stay with you forever.

4. Vancouver Korean-Canadian Scholarship Foundation

I became elected to be chair of the scholarship foundation by its board of directors in January 2002, following the foundation's evolvement from being a program run by the Vancouver Korean Association to becoming its own independent entity. I'd never imagined I would hold such a position, but the idea of supporting the next generation of Korean-Canadians resonated with me, and I accepted the role. I began my work with this organization 20 years ago at the age of 55 after spending the previous decade building my financial foundation. When I commit to something, I tend to pour all my energy into it, as if in a fever, and the work I was doing with the foundation soon became something I was very passionate about.

The purpose of our organization is to identify and award scholarships to qualified students who have demonstrated academic excellence and show promise of taking leadership roles in the Korean community and Canadian society. We want to encourage these students to develop their talents and realize their dreams and help them both financially and by providing networking opportunities.

Fundraising is critical to operating a scholarship foundation, so when I took the helm, I was especially concerned about this area of our activities. Our aim was to provide as many students as possible with as many scholarships as possible, and we aggressively moved forward toward this goal. Each scholarship would be named for the organization, business, or individual who had donated the funds to create it, and we ensured that every dollar of that donation was being awarded to the recipient. During my tenure as chair, I took care of all of the administrative costs. When we began, we awarded $300 to seven students; by 2018, we had awarded $1,045,500 to 759 students and were managing a fund of about $300,000.

After two years, I was exhausted, and there was talk of making the foundation private, so I asked Lee Ken-Beck to take over, which he did in 2004, and then I took over again in 2005. UBC professor Kim Hyo-shin was chair from 2009 to 2011, and Hur Namlin, also a professor at UBC, led the foundation from 2012 until 2013, when I returned to the role once again. In 2019, Kim Ji-hoon, an attorney, became chair and was succeeded in 2021 by Kim Bum-seok, a pharmacist, who is chair of the foundation currently, while I help behind the scenes as a board member.

One of my memorable experiences as chair was organizing a charity concert featuring Jo Young-nam. At the time, Mr. Jo had a friendly relationship with my husband, having read his book, which he described as having spiritually liberated him, and begun a correspondence. So, I was able to ask whether he would be willing to headline a charity event for us, and fortunately, he agreed to lend us his support. He said it was the first time in his life that he was performing at a concert for free.

We booked the 2,765-seat Queen Elizabeth Theatre, one of Vancouver's largest performing arts venue, for the concert. Today, the local Korean community is much larger, but back then there were only around 20,000 people. A Joo Hyun-mi concert around that time had filled around 700 seats. In hindsight, I recognize how reckless it was to book such a large venue, but I was confident we were going to put on the biggest and most amazing show and was determined to go all out to make it happen. I approached all the Korean churches in the area, distributing 100 tickets at each one to sell to their congregants, and went out personally into the Korean community to sell tickets.

Not a moment went smoothly during preparations for the event. At the time, my husband was becoming well known for his book No Such Jesus, and some churches, misunderstanding the book's message, refused to help me sell tickets. As well, this was around the time of the 2002 FIFA World Cup, when the South Korean team made its historic run, and it was looking like the date of the concert was going to conflict with the quarterfinals. And I was constantly on edge, because it was just days before the concert and only 1,500 of the tickets had been sold. Then, on top of everything, one of Jo Young-nam's band members was being detained at the airport due to a miscommunication with border officials.

I still break out in a sweat when I think about all the running back and forth between the airport and the Korean consulate and the last-minute ticket sales. As luck would have it, South

Korea's quarterfinal match was
scheduled for June 21, 2002,
the day before the concert, so
the excitement of reaching the
quarterfinals had the effect of
uniting the Korean community.
All of the seats were filled, we
sang along, hugged each other,
cried, and had an emotional
time. It was an experience
difficult to describe with words,
and I can only say that the heavens saved me.

The show was so successful I was receiving requests to bring
over other celebrities, perhaps Lee Mi-ja. I don't know anything
about show business, but it was fun. We also held a harbor
cruise event with Jo Young-nam, and although tickets were $200
per person, there was such demand, it was another important
opportunity for further fundraising. In total, we were able to raise
$60,000 for the scholarship fund.

There were many helping hands to achieve such good results.
I am grateful to Kim Young-il, who personally bought tickets for
the entire front row, the staffers at the Korean consulate who were
able to extract the band members from the airport, and members
of the Korean community who filled the concert hall. I still get
teary-eyed with gratitude, and I believe that it was all of us
together who were supporting the hopes and dreams of so many

Korean students.

Mr. Jo was happy to spend time with us, staying up the night before his return flight to talk. He was still somewhat inebriated when it was time to catch his flight in the morning. I patted him on the back and got him on his plane just in time. Despite all its challenges, the experience of putting on this concert is still a precious memory to me: in many ways, including financially, it represented the launch of the foundation.

Another memorable experience was preparing for "scholarship night," which we viewed not only as an awards ceremony but also as an opportunity to raise the Korean community's profile in Canada's mainstream society. We knew how important it was to have dialog between our communities, so we held a lavish event every year, inviting MLAs, MPs, and cabinet ministers, as well as representatives from other ethnic communities and Korean-Canadian public figures. The program included Korean folk dance, musical performances, charity auctions, and raffles.

For our first awards ceremony, we reserved a banquet hall with a capacity of 500 people at the Hilton Hotel in Burnaby and began inviting practically every political public figure I could think of, in the hopes that our students could meet them. Additionally, there were very few occasions at the time for Korean-Canadians to get all dressed up and gather, so I wanted to create such an event.

Putting on such an event was a huge undertaking, and it was unlike anything I'd ever done before. There was a lot to prepare for. We needed to create a detailed event itinerary, solicit comments from each of the recipients to include them in the program, and make sure that the performers had everything they needed. Other tasks included making name tags and coming up with a seating arrangement that would facilitate conversation among the guests. I felt like even a year would not have been

enough time to get everything ready. In the month leading up to
the event, I was working nonstop, with little time to eat or sleep.
I would often send emails in the middle of the night and the

recipients would respond asking, when do you ever sleep?

We were having to accommodate requests from attendees to change where they were seated, which we were happy to do, but these requests were coming in up to and including the day of the event, so there was no respite. In the end, however, everybody seemed happy at the event, which is of course what we wanted. We also paid very close attention to where the students were seated, wanting to give them the opportunity to interact with potential mentors in their fields.

It has been immensely fulfilling to have been able to support our students with resources that will help them succeed in Canadian society and make an impact. It is a worthwhile cause and something I have poured my heart and soul into without taking a day off. Since those early days, scholarship night has evolved, the evening now includes a charity auction, and the scale of donations has grown. I hope there will eventually be a culture of donating like there is in other countries.

If I had to do it over again, I would willingly do it, because it is my mission as an instrument of God. Everything I have has been entrusted to me by God, and I believe I should use it as He intended. In addition, it has been supremely gratifying to see our scholarship recipients go on to thrive and make a difference in the world. I think my desire to provide a nurturing environment for the next generation to grow up healthy and strong is the driving force behind this work for me.

Dr. Yeon Eun-soon, a cultural reporter for the Vancouver

JoongAng Ilbo, wrote an article about me that was published on page 17 of the newspaper's November 23, 2002, issue.

The ever-blue moonlight, the river of deep love: Oh Yoo-soon, chair of the Vancouver Korean-Canadian Scholarship Foundation By Yeon Eun-soon "Scholarships are not charity but an invaluable investment for the future."

1. On a rainy night, gazing in the blue moonlight

A glimpse of clear sky on a rainy night. A half-moon glides across, its light shining through. It is mysterious and eerie. On the other hand, it is also familiar. I look up for a long time, captivated by its cool and dignified appearance. My whole body seems to have been cleansed by the baptism in moonlight. Even my soul seems to have been cleansed.

If the sun is masculine, the moon is the feminine symbol. Although the moon seems lyrical and weak, it envelops us with more subtlety than the intense sun. On nights when we have lost our light, when we weep with disappointment and despair, on nights when we are weary with loneliness and want to rest, the eternal mother goddess soothes us and embraces us with infinite warmth. She is the one who will forever receive our tears. Who hasn't relied on the moon to soothe their loneliness? Who hasn't had the moon as a friend while walking along the road in the dark night?

Have you ever been hungry, lying alone in a cold room,

staring up at the heavens in awe, thinking about the steaming dumplings you once ate, or the white rice you scooped into the bowl?

Have you ever shed tears due to poverty? Have you ever walked around the school and wiped away tears with your fists because of an overdue tuition payment? How many times have you said to yourself that poverty is not something to be ashamed of, just an inconvenience, but do you remember that lonely scene from your childhood when you were made to be acutely aware that it was not only inconvenient but also embarrassing? Do you remember the moonlight that was always there, its unchanging blue? Do you remember the warmth of the moonlight?

There is a person who wants to give in return for the love she has received, and always shines with the radiance and splendor of the blue moonlight. There is a person who embraces everyone with gentleness and warmth: Oh Yoo-soon, chair of the Vancouver Korean-Canadian Scholarship Foundation.

On the way back from our meeting, I saw the moon had risen exceptionally high in the sky and illuminated the whole world. The last line from Faust, the Eternal Feminine draws us onward evermore, came to mind. It was a rainy night in early winter.

2. The Eternal Feminine draws us onward

Oh Yoo-soon, influenced by her father who worked in the pharmaceutical industry, applied to the college of pharmacy for university. After completing graduate school in South Korea, she got married to Oh Kang-nam and they immigrated to Canada as students. It was 1971, and they first settled in Hamilton, Ontario, where her husband's school was located. Having already earned her master's degree in pharmacy in South Korea, she wanted to continue her studies, but thought it would be better to first obtain her license to practice as her husband was still a student and they were parents to a newborn at the time. She completed the required coursework at the University of Toronto's Faculty of Pharmacy and became a licensed pharmacist in Ontario. Due to her husband's career, she then moved to Toronto; Winnipeg, Manitoba; Edmonton, Alberta; and Regina, Saskatchewan, where she worked as a pharmacy manager. Provinces in Canada do not recognize pharmacist's licenses from other provinces, so whenever she relocated, she had to take the qualification exam once again, which is why she has five licenses to practice in five provinces. Living all across Canada has also taught her the benefits of nomadic living, and she made good friends in each city. Life is a journey after all.

It was never going to be easy to study, work as a pharmacist, and take care of young children, all while getting adjusted to a new life in a new country with no family around, but it was particularly difficult when it was time to drop off her children at daycare because they wouldn't want to leave their mother's arms and she couldn't bear to leave them. She couldn't help but shed tears too. To this day, she gets teary-eyed when she looks back on those days. There were inevitably moments of such conflict, but they made her stronger and made her recognize the preciousness of human life.

The only child of a wealthy family, Ms. Oh grew up in a life of privilege. Her parents had always believed their abundance should be shared with everyone and not just for them to enjoy. Her maternal grandfather was Christian and active as a religious leader, and her father had an especially generous nature and believed that just because he had earned his money that didn't mean it should all be his, so it was natural to share with neighbors and family members. He put his beliefs into practice. Although she was raised in an affluent environment, her actions as an adult did not reflect that upbringing. She was the one to take on the dirty jobs at large gatherings or when doing volunteer work with her school. She grew up enjoying having many things but did not forget that she should give back to others for the grace she had received.

Raised to be a devout Christian, she strived for spiritual growth, but at the age of 30, she fell into a period of serious reflection on religion and her life. During this time, she experienced many moments of epiphany and joy through meditation. Afterward, she felt even more strongly that people were lovely, and she wanted to help them. This unusual experience made her more serious about her life and it filled her with love.

Her definition of life is rather unusual. She believes that her purpose in this world is to develop her own divinity and to leave this world having helped it. This philosophy of life may be what makes her love for her neighbors so extraordinary.

In August 2000, by which time her children were all grown and she had some time on her hands, she joined the board of the Vancouver Korean-Canadian Scholarship Foundation. It was a natural progression for her, as she was already helping orphans and had thought she would devote her life to the service of others when the time came. She always had a plan for her life: work on her education until age 25, work for her children's education until age 45, establish a financial foundation until age 55, and then focus on a life of working for the public good.

3. Pure and unadulterated, the source of the water

In 1999, the scholarship foundation, which had been established as a program by the Vancouver Korean Association, became its own entity as the Vancouver Korean-Canadian Scholarship Foundation, and in December 2001, Ms. Oh became chair. In January 2002, the organization applied to become a registered charity and received a registration number from the Canadian government. In June 2002, the nonprofit hosted a charity concert headlined by Jo Young-nam, which was well received by many people. Currently 11 board members actively work together to raise funds. They have been able to award scholarships to 29 students this year, up

from seven in 1999, the organization's first year. The Korean community has come to trust the foundation and continues to donate generously. Some individuals have chosen to donate large sums anonymously. This year, there are seven newly established scholarships, including ones from South Korea's Kyungdong Pharmaceutical and HSBC Bank, and the number of scholarships is expected to continue to increase in coming years. This is indeed encouraging.

The purpose of the foundation is to provide scholarships to university students of Korean heritage who have a record of academic excellence, a history of community service, and financial need. "Scholarships are not charity but an invaluable investment for the future," says Ms. Oh. "Let's do our best to encourage our children who are facing various challenges such as language barriers, cultural differences, and racial issues and help them realize their dreams."

Ms. Oh currently operates a pharmacy in Coquitlam. Seeing people come into her pharmacy with minor ailments, such as sniffles, has made her think differently about disease and our lives. "Health is not only about physical health but also about mental health," she says. Just as a medicine can function as a medicine if used correctly but become poison if used improperly, so can our actions and our lives if we do not find our place. She believes that all of the money she earns is not hers alone, and that it is natural to give back to society what she has. The scholarship foundation is very important to her in that sense. She firmly believes that it is a good place for realizing her dreams.

Her soul is bright and filled with grace. It is transparent and pure, and it purifies the hearts of those around her. She is sincere with everyone, and this sincerity has the power to touch people's hearts. She is like a loving healer tending to a broken soul. Those who meet her remember her innocence and warmth long afterwards. They remember her as a beautiful soul who wants to give back to others the love and benefits she has received. She is a rare person who puts her thoughts into practice. She reminds me of the French philosopher Simone de Beauvoir, who moved people with her extraordinary love of her neighbors. Her existence is like a clean water source in this harsh world of industrialization. How many souls have been comforted by Antoine de Saint Exupery's The Little Prince. Her soul is indeed no different than that of the Little Prince.

When life is hard, I will remember her, and I will call her, for she is surely precious. I will listen to her clear voice and look forward to tomorrow anew. On a night in early winter, the moonlight still shines through the window.

5. Campaign against repatriation of North Korean refugees

When I first read that North Korean refugees were being forcibly repatriated by the Chinese government, my heart sank. I have heard that the North Korean government severely punishes those who try to defect with imprisonment, torture, and forced labor under inhumane conditions. Then in 2012 the case of a North Korean refugee captured in Changchun sparked a movement against forced repatriation. In Vancouver, more than 300 members of the Korean community, both young and old, braved the rain and cold, to protest in front of the Chinese embassy. We also collected signatures for a petition, and within a month and a half we had 10,000 signatures. These were not due to one person's efforts but rather the result of a collaboration between the Vancouver Korean Association, the East Sea Veterans Association, the Korean War Veterans Association, members of the business community, the Advisory Committee for Peaceful Reunification, and numerous religious organizations. We realized that even though our individual voices were small, if we all came together and spoke as one, we could send a powerful message that would be heard not only by the Canadian government but by nations around the world. This unity was even more meaningful because it was for justice and peace.

We sent a statement expressing the views of the Korean

Protest in support of North Korean refugees in front of the Chinese embassy in Vancouver.

community to Prime Minister Harper through Senator Martin and secured a formal meeting with minister of citizenship and immigration Jason Kenney to discuss the issue. We also sent the 10,000 signatures we collected to the United Nations in an effort to have the international community recognize and intervene in the North Korean refugee crisis. The hope was that every country in the world would recognize the peril facing North Korean refugees and take them in.

I went to the 12th World Summit of Nobel Peace Laureates in Chicago to personally deliver a letter explaining the plight of North Korean refugees and expressing our opposition to the Chinese government's forced repatriation of these refugees. I attended the forum dressed in a hanbok to identify myself as a Korean, and I met with several attendees individually to ask them to stand with us. Many Nobel Peace laureates were sympathetic, and 190 people signed our petition, including former Polish president Lech Walesa.

I was moved that the world would care about North Koreans and hoped that North Korea could become a peaceful country that respected human rights. Meeting former US president Jimmy Carter, former Soviet president Mikhail Gorbachev, the Dalai Lama, whom I have long wanted to meet, and actor Sean Penn, with whom I took a picture, was inspiring, showing me how one person can make a difference in the lives of so many. I hope that I can pass on this impact that meeting them had on me.

The World Summit is a forum in which Nobel Peace laureates

and stakeholders can come together to address global issues with a view to making progress toward world peace. I have been attending for several years, starting with the 2010 summit, which was held in Hiroshima, Japan, as part of my role with the World Peace Foundation. The discussions, ranging in topic from peace and social and economic justice to the rule of law and environmental and sustainable development, have opened my eyes to what is happening in other parts of the world. In particular, I was able to interact closely with Mairead Corrigan Maguire, Shirin Ebadi, and Jody Williams, all of whose life stories are inspirational to me. I realized that as much as we need the international community to know about what is happening to North Korean refugees, we should do our part for the international community.

The 18th World Summit will be held in Pyeongchang. I hope it will be opportunity for the two Koreas, which bear the scars of

war and division, to have dialog and lay the foundation for peace on the Korean peninsula. I pray that the rights of the people of North Korea will be recognized and protected, and I will continue to spread the word in the international community and do all that I can until that day comes. As the Dalai Lama teaches, I want to value love, compassion, forgiveness, and peace, and prioritize loving people until the day when all people in the world live in peace.

6. Helping North Korean children

My involvement in feeding starving children in North Korea began when I became a board member of First Steps, a Vancouver-based nonprofit founded by Susan Ritchie. The organization's primary purpose is to prevent child malnutrition in North Korea through programs that provide essential nutrients to young children. Our work included shipping soybeans, food processing equipment, and prenatal nutrition to the country.

The driving force behind this work was Susan Ritchie. Before starting First Steps, she had traveled to North Korea as an interpreter for a Canadian government delegation, so she had contacts that were vital to our activities there. Also, she had grown up in South Korea as her parents were missionaries, and this gave her a deep understanding of the Korean language and culture. As I watched from the sidelines, her dedication made me think, here was someone who deserved a Nobel Prize.

As part of its operations, First Steps visited North Korea four times per year to confirm that its shipments of soybeans were reaching the children for whom they were intended and not being diverted elsewhere. It also visited schools, orphanages, and daycares to observe the distribution of the soymilk and monitor and report on the children's growth.

The organization now ships soybeans purchased in Canada and South Korea, but in the early years we were buying them from

Chinese suppliers and were running into problems with these suppliers mixing sand in with the beans in order to deceive the weigh scales or intercepting shipments before they reached their destinations. So Ms. Ritchie and others would have to travel to North Korea to oversee their operations there, despite the dangers. I was able to accompany her on several of these occasions and I will never forget the experience.

In 2002, Ms. Ritchie, myself, and five other Canadians traveled to North Korea and various locations within the country, including Hyongjesan, Pyongyang, and Wonsan, to visit daycares. It was a special opportunity since most visitors were limited to seeing only Pyongyang. But getting into North Korea was not easy. First, we had to travel to China, where I would have to wait to be approved for a visa enabling me to enter the country. The wait was nerve wracking; if I was refused, I would have to return to South Korea. During that time, I visited a market and purchased a few items, like sweaters, to distribute to North Koreans.

Eventually my visa application was approved, and we boarded a plane bound for North Korea along with many other passengers who were traveling there to help in all sorts of ways. It was heartwarming to see people of so many different nationalities. It also greatened my sense of responsibility for my countrymen. There was a moment of concern when my cellphone and passport were taken at the airport, but I was encouraged by the example of the people on the plane with me.

It was an emotional experience landing at Sunan International

Airport. In addition to the excitement for what lay ahead, I was saddened that it was 2002 and it looked like the place was still in the 1950s. There would be many moments during this trip when I would have to hide my tears or be unable to smile upon seeing the poor conditions.

From the airport, we went to a hotel in Pyongyang. The neighborhood surrounding the hotel had no electricity, so it was difficult to walk around after dark without a flashlight, but the golf course next door was a place of luxury where one could hit golf balls into the Taedong River. The restaurant where we had dinner served fine dining, and the prices were similar to those you would find in Canada. In a country where starvation was rampant, it was uncomfortable to see such luxury that only a tiny percentage had the wealth to enjoy. I prayed that one day soon North Korea would be able to take care of its poor.

For most of the trip I was accompanied by a guide, but in the early mornings I had the chance to walk around the neighborhood on my own. So, I went out with the sweaters I'd bought, but when I tried to give them to people, they would refuse. I found out later that people were required to travel in pairs so that one could report the other for any infractions. I was saddened to learn that even friendly interactions between neighbors could be so tightly controlled. It made me question whether true happiness could exist in a country that didn't respect personal freedom. The next day, I approached people who were by themselves walking along the road or next to a creek and quietly offered them the sweaters.

Seeing their faces light up with gratitude, I could breathe a sigh of relief. I still have one of those sweaters from that time, and every time I wear it, it brings back memories of my time in North Korea.

We traveled from Pyongyang to Hyongjaesan in a small van we'd bought. We visited a daycare there and there were children who were 10 years old but less than a meter in height, their growth stunted by malnutrition. Some of them had the energy to move around, but others just lay there. When I saw that, my heart broke and I cried. I didn't expect to ever see such suffering. They were children, they should be running around and playing, but they didn't have the energy to sit up. It was difficult to look in their faces. I don't think anybody could have been there and not wanted to help.

We confirmed there was a supply of soymilk at the location and weighed and measured the children to monitor their progress. From Canada, we had sent two types of soymilk-producing machines, one that was fueled by wood, coal, or corn cobs and one that ran on electricity. Because electricity was so scarce in the area, the electric machines were practically useless.

From the daycare, we traveled to Wonsan, a coastal city surrounded by dense pine forest. When I learned that a modern facility there was being used as a camp for the children of high-ranking government officials, I suggested to our guide that the place could be converted into a resort for international travelers, which would bring in foreign currency that could be used to alleviate the suffering of ordinary North Koreans. At the Koryo

Hotel, I was again surprised to see the restaurant had the lights on for the benefit of the few people in our group, as even Pyongyang had hardly any electricity. I thought that such a place would greatly benefit the tourism industry, if there were one. I considered how North Korea could lift itself out of poverty without relying on foreign aid.

At the restaurant, I met a North Korean woman who proposed that we work together on a business. She was a sophisticated woman who had been able to travel abroad freely because she was the daughter of a high-ranking official. She said there were no cakes in North Korea, so if we made cakes -- wedding cakes, birthday cakes, cakes for other occasions -- we could have a successful business. I didn't expect to receive such a proposal in North Korea, so I found it special to listen as she explained how the flour would be milled and how the cakes would be made. Although nothing further developed from our conversation, I am hopeful that North Korea's economic development can benefit from people like her who have foreign experience.

Afterwards, we visited Kim Il-sung's mausoleum, which is a grand building with a long escalator. Many of the women present were dressed in hanboks and crying. In many places around North Korea, the citizens bowed as if worshiping a god, but Ms. Ritchie never did, so we didn't either. We were outsiders receiving special leeway, but nevertheless the fact that she stood up for herself in the face of oppression left a deep impression on us.

At Myohyangsan, there is a building that houses the many gifts

At Mount Kumgang, circa 2004.

Kim Il-sung received from other heads of states, among them South Korean presidents. After a tour of the collection, we were led outside to a park where a mat had been spread for a picnic, and I noticed our guide was shivering from the cold, so I gave him my overcoat. He was very touched by this very small gesture and repeatedly expressed his gratitude during the remainder of my stay. It had taken a few days to become acquainted, but after warming up to each other we realized we were all one people.

There was one thing I was anxious about throughout much of my trip. When leaving Canada, I had packed antibiotics and

painkillers that were difficult to come by in North Korea. Upon arriving at the airport in Pyongyang, I gave the medications to our North Korean guides with the request that they deliver them to where they could be put to good use. However, in the following days, they never mentioned anything about the medications, which made me uneasy. I wondered whether I had done something wrong or if something had gone wrong and I would be detained in North Korea. On the last night of our visit, as we said goodbye to our guides, one of them cried and expressed his gratitude for the medicine, saying it would help hundreds of people. They had been too cautious to speak of it earlier, but the words were now coming out with the help of alcohol the night before my departure. You can't imagine how relieved I felt to hear this. How fortunate that the medicine would be used to help people. As a pharmacist, I was pleased to be able to treat North Koreans. Since my visit, I have continued to send medicine to North Korea. I hope that soon I will be able to do so freely.

I took many photographs to document my visit, but almost all of them were deleted, and I had to return home with only memories. I will not forget eating my favorite cold noodles by the Taedong River. I will carry my memories of North Korea in my heart. They are particularly special because North Korea is my grandfather's homeland. I believe he was watching from heaven, happy that I was able to visit. I look forward to the day when North and South Koreans can come and go as they please and all the separated families can embrace each other once again.

On August 27, 2009, Yonhap reporter Kang Jin-wook interviewed me for a feature story titled Korean Women in the World. Most of the events detailed in the interview are already contained in this memoir, but I'm including it here for reference.

Korean women in the world
By Kang Jin-wook

There is a woman who has been working as a pharmacist for 38 years in Canada while serving as a godmother to the Korean community by providing scholarships and volunteering for various activities.

After immigrating to the country with her husband as students in 1971 and obtaining her pharmacist's license, she lived in five provinces before settling in British Columbia, where she has been operating Eagle Ridge Drugs, also known as Oh Yoo Soon Pharmacy, for the past 18 years.

She has been a board member of the Vancouver Korean-Canadian Scholarship Foundation for more than 10 years and became chair last year. A total of 376 students have been awarded scholarships since 1999. Canadian students pursuing academic studies related to Korea at a Canadian university such as the University of British Columbia are also eligible. The scholarships range from $1,000 up to, in the case of financial need, $5,000. The scholarship fund has reached a total of $300,000, which includes a $20,000 donation from HSBC Bank. Ms. Oh has also established a scholarship in her name, the Oh Yoo-soon Scholarship. She actively encourages her peers to donate in their name and has fundraised alumni scholarships from Korean universities, such as Seoul National University and Ewha Womans University.

She has been involved in various volunteer work since immigrating to Canada. This year she founded the Rose of Sharon Foundation. The purpose of the organization is to take care of elderly Koreans living in Canada. "At my pharmacy, I see many elderly Korean-Canadians who are no longer able to be cared for by their families, yet they don't want to go into a Canadian nursing home because of the language barrier and the food doesn't suit them," she says. "The situation is very serious." She relates the story of one elderly Korean-Canadian who entered a Canadian care facility and refused to eat, choosing to end his own life. "We need to create an environment of mutual support, whether that's through creating charities or volunteering, so that the Korean community can thrive in Canada."

"It takes money to build a nursing home," she says. "So, we are holding bazaars. We raised $4,000 through sales in June and last month a Korean food event we held at UBC raised $3,000. At the most recent 8.15 bazaar, we raised a whopping $40,000. Right now, we are in the middle of preparing for a charity concert with the Zion Choir taking place next month."

With word of her activities spreading and her profile rising in the community, Canadian prime minister Stephen Harper recently directed one of his aides to reach out and encourage her to run for parliament. "I had no intention of going into politics, and I thought it would be better for someone from the younger generation to step in rather than me, an old person, so I recommended somebody else," she says. "I don't want to take on anything complicated," she replies when asked whether she would ever want to enter politics. Even within the Korean community, there are many people recommending her for this or that opportunity, but she declines them all. Prime Minister Harper has continued to express his support for the Korean community and made a visit to the scholarship foundation of which she is a board member.

When asked about the political influence of the Korean-

Canadian community, she replies, "I'm very hopeful." Yonah Martin (45, Korean name Kim Yeon-ah), who became the first Canadian of Korean descent to be appointed to the Senate of Canada, is a prime example. She calls Ms. Oh her "mentor." "I feel that the Canadian government would pay more attention to the Korean-Canadian community if more Korean-Canadians became engaged in politics," Ms. Oh says.

To this end, she is working diligently to help secure internships for second-generation Korean-Canadians with the offices of members of parliament and has currently placed three interns. Most of them plan to continue to work for these politicians after the end of their internships to further their political education. "We also have a number of second-generation Korean-Canadians who are excelling in various other fields, such as lawyers, doctors, and computer engineers. It will be interesting to see what they do in the future."

As the Korean-Canadian community's influence grows, so does its power. With the support of Senator Martin, Ms. Oh recently petitioned the Canadian government to launch a Meals on Wheels program to deliver Korean food to elderly Koreans in need. "With Yonah Martin and Barry Devolin serving as co-chairs of the Conservative Party's Korean-Canadian task force, I think we're going to see a lot of programs for Koreans soon."

In addition to the scholarship program and a Korean nursing home, Ms. Oh would like to build a Korean cultural center this year. "For Koreans to maintain their identity, we must not forget our culture and traditions, but there is no facility in Canada, and I hope the Korean government will help."

Ms. Oh has been senior vice president of the Western Chapter of the Peaceful Unification Advisory Council since 2003 and a board member of First Steps, a Canadian non-profit dedicated to helping North Korean children, since 2006.

Photo wall
Wall display in the lobby of the Eunice Oh Residence

EUNICE YOO SOON OH KANG
LIFETIME ACHIEVEMENTS

EDUCATION

1959-1965	Kyunggi Girls' Middle and High School
1965-1969	BPharm, Ewha Womans University College of Pharmacy
1969-1971	MPharm, Ewha Womans University College of Pharmacy
1975-1976	University of Toronto Faculty of Pharmacy
1976-	Pharmacist's licenses in Ontario, Manitoba, Saskatchewan, Alberta, and British Columbia

AWARDS

2004	Award for excellence in social service from the prime minister of the Republic of Korea
2007	Gwanak Award, Seoul National University Alumni Association in Vancouver
2010	Awards for excellence in community service from the president of the Republic of Korea
2012	Plaque of appreciation, Korean War Veterans Association in Vancouver
2012	Queen Elizabeth II Diamond Jubilee Medal, Government of Canada
2013	Plaque of appreciation, Korean War Veterans Association of the Republic of Korea
2017	Senate 150th Anniversary Medal
2022	Winner, APOthecary Heroes of Canada Contest
2023	Certificate of appreciation, Ewha Womans University College of Pharmacy Alumnae Association in Korea

COMMUNITY SERVICE

2002-2003	Chair, Vancouver Korean-Canadian Scholarship Foundation
2003	President, Kyunggi Girls' High School Alumnae Association in Vancouver
2003-2011	First vice president, The Peaceful Unification Advisory Council, Vancouver Chapter
2003-2011	Chair, Women's Committee, The Peaceful Unification Advisory Council, Vancouver Chapter
2004-2006	Consultant, Q&A on pharmaceutical- and health-related matters, Vancouver Chosun Daily Press
2005-2008	Chair, Vancouver Korean-Canadian Scholarship Foundation
2006-2015	Board member, First Steps, an organization committed to preventing child malnutrition in North Korea
2009-	Chair, Rose of Sharon Foundation
2009-2010	President, Rose of Sharon Care Society
2009-2012	President, Korean Society of British Columbia for Fraternity & Culture
2011-2013	President, The Ewha Womans University Alumnae Association in Vancouver
2012	President, The Ewha Womans University Alumnae Association of North America
2012-2014	Member, The Multicultural Advisory Council, BC, Canada
2013	Chair, The Ewha Womans University Alumnae Association of North America
2013-2023	Member, The Peaceful Unification Advisory Council, Vancouver Chapter
2014-2018	Chair, The Vancouver Korean-Canadian Scholarship Foundation
2014-	Board of Directors, The Vancouver Korean-Canadian Scholarship Foundation
2017	Board of Directors, The New Vista Society

Eunice (Yoo Soon) Oh was born in South Korea and immigrated to Canada in 1971.

Eunice is pictured with the Honourable George Furey, who was then the speaker of the Senate of Canada, and Senator

Founder and president of Oh Pharmacy, Eunice was named a winner of the first APOthecary Heroes Contest in 2022 in recognition of her outstanding contributions as a pharmacy professional in Canada.

She is married with three sons, two daughters-in-law and four grandsons(parents pictured above left, family pictured above right)

Among her many other philanthropic enterprises, Eunice helped establish the Vancouver Korean-Canadian Scholarship Foundation to promote and encourage academic excellence among students of Korean heritage. As of 2022, the foundation has awarded over $1.4 million in scholarships for postsecondary education. The Right Honourable Stephen Harper, who was then the prime minister of Canada, attended the foundation's inaugural award ceremony.

Yonah Martin at the awarding of her Senate 150th Anniversary Medal for her leadership and contribution to the Korean community of British Columbia in 2017.

In November 2020, Eunice realized a lifelong dream of supporting a venue to provide culturally sensitive care to Korean-Canadians. At the New Vista Care Home (left), the second floor is dedicated to providing Korean meals, entertainment, and Korean-speaking caregivers for 40 residents. She donated $1 million to help achieve this goal.

Chapter 2 :

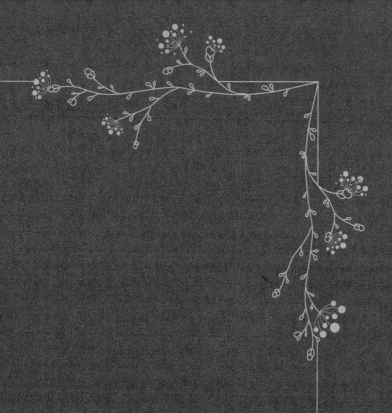

Immigrant
life

1. Pharmacy management

Pharmacy is one of my greatest passions. My life ambition was to operate my own pharmacy, so I studied pharmacy in university, created a differentiated pharmacy management system, and spent most of my younger years in a pharmacy. To me, a pharmacy is a way to help sick people with medication, a place to gather with neighbors, and an asset for my family to fulfill our dreams.

April 1, 1992, holds a special place in my heart as it marks the day when my pharmacy first opened its doors. Even after all these years, I can still vividly recall the excitement and mixed emotions I experienced when I finally had my own pharmacy after working at others for so long. I remember going around by myself to set everything up, choosing the location, leasing the space, and ordering the stock. To save money, I bought used shelves at a supplier on Schoolhouse Street in Coquitlam. I cleaned and refinished them to make them look brand new and installed them myself. Around the same time, Park Woo-sam was starting his own laundromat business in a unit across the way, and watching all of this he probably thought my efforts were extreme. When the day finally arrived for the pharmacy to open, people began to come in. The shelves were not even filled, but seeing all the people seeking medications moved my heart. Isn't it said that dreams are meant to be fulfilled? For me, this was a dream come true, the day when all my hard work was paying off.

Starting a pharmacy wasn't easy. This was around when pharmacies were starting to open in large grocery stores, and many small pharmacies were going out of business. After moving to the area, I was looking around for where I could start my business and eventually found the perfect spot adjacent to some medical offices. There was also a hospital close by, and it was in Coquitlam, near my home. However, before I signed the lease, the doctors at the medical offices tried to discourage me from going through with it, because two previous pharmacies in that location had failed. Despite their warnings, I signed anyway with the mindset, "Even if I fail, I will start here!" I had a youthful passion, but I also had 18 years of experience and knew all the ins and outs of running a pharmacy. I was confident in my ability to make it successful because I had seen firsthand how it was done.

The main problem was that I didn't have a license to practice pharmacy in British Columbia yet. The qualification exam in BC is notoriously difficult, to the extent that many pharmacists in other parts of Canada are hesitant to move there. Basically, it was a test you failed four times before passing, but I signed the lease without even having taken it once. It was a reckless risk: I signed the lease with a planned opening date in April and was scheduled to take the exam in February. It was a lot of pressure, but I managed to pass on my first try. I was able to overcome this obstacle and open my pharmacy as planned, so how can I say that it wasn't by the grace of God?

In the beginning, I worked at the pharmacy by myself without a staff because I remembered how difficult it was to manage employees when I was a manager at a large pharmacy. Although I was running it by myself, I was doing the work of three people, and my husband and my sons would help during school vacations, so it was not a big problem. My dedication to the pharmacy paid off, and despite my initial fears, Eagle Ridge Drugs became a place where more and more people came to visit. I tried to maintain my smile and my friendliness, because I thought a pharmacy should be not only for selling medicine but also a place to meet people. I loved meeting people, too, so the pharmacy quickly became known as a community pharmacy, even though we had very few Korean customers.

I also operated as a dispensary, which focused on hospital prescriptions. Pharmacies in Canada are like grocery stores, selling all kinds of different things, but I wanted to specialize in medicines. When I first came to Canada in 1971 and started working as a pharmacy technician, I would take orders over the phone, and I would have trouble understanding words like "Rothmans" (a brand of cigarettes) and "Jersey Milk" (a kind of chocolate bar), so I used to get confused about whether they wanted cigarettes or chocolate. I'd come a long way since then, and I could not only understand the pronunciations but also read the doctors' scrawled prescriptions and I felt that was because of my accumulated experience. My heart was filled with excitement and hope because I had my own pharmacy specializing in medicine.

I was very attentive to the customers who came in. I thought their health should come first, not selling medicine. If a customer came in looking for vitamins because they felt their health was declining, my first thought wasn't to sell them vitamins but rather to encourage them to exercise more and eat more fruits and vegetables. Perhaps this approach got through to them, because sometimes a customer after coming in only once and then moving away would make a special trip to the pharmacy to buy their medicine.

The staff at Eagle Ridge Hospital liked the pharmacy so much it became their go-to supplier. The hospital not only came to me for their prescription needs, but the pharmacy was its designated supplier of palliative emergency kits. These kits contain medications used for symptoms at the end of life, many of which are narcotics, such as morphine, which requires careful management. So, it was a sign of their trust in me that only my pharmacy would be the one to manage their supply of palliative emergency kits.

This was also when we started making blister packs. The packs made it easier for patients to track their medications, dividing the pills by what time of the day when they should be taken, which was especially useful for elderly patients taking multiple medications. The service became so popular that doctors in other parts of the country would ask me how they could appropriately provide this kind of care for their patients.

The pharmacy was open on Christmas and New Year's Day,

when all the others in the area were closed for the holidays. On these days, even though I was working as quickly as I could, there was often a line out the door. And for people with limited mobility, I had available delivery. Nowadays, pharmacies commonly stay open even on major holidays, so it's no longer necessary for me to keep mine open at all hours. It was difficult to work without any holidays, but at the time, I wanted to help people who needed their medications, so I was able to work despite the difficulties.

Another service I provided was dispensing methadone. Methadone is a medication used to treat opioid addiction, and, under a government-administered program, patients can come into the pharmacy each day to take their methadone dose. I had to be careful because some of the patients could be a little rough-mannered, but I provided the service with a sense of mission. So, even during those times when I had to be firm with patients who were demanding more than what was prescribed, I think they could sense my sincerity and respect for them, and they would comply.

Pharmacies deal with narcotics, however, so there have been robberies. In one incident, a robber dressed in a Halloween costume came in through the back door of a drug store I was working at. He was carrying pepper spray and demanded I open the medicine cabinet, so I opened the cabinet, and he ran away with the drugs. A Korean customer who happened to be there at the time saw this and ran after the robber, screaming for people to catch him, but it was Halloween, so people thought it was a prank.

Eventually the robber was arrested, and the crucial evidence was that the pills were marked with the pharmacy's identifier. There was a similar incident when I lived in Regina. After these experiences, I make sure all of my pills are marked, and I wanted my pharmacy to have no back door and its dispensing area to have a secure entry.

In Regina, I had an encounter with a robber armed with a gun and wanting drugs. It was a larger store, so we had a security guard, but the robber came in when the guard was on a coffee break. In the heat of the moment, I thought I would stall until the guard returned, so I asked the robber, "What do you want?" even though it was obvious what he wanted. He told me to open the safe and I complied but as slowly as I could and asked again, "What exactly do you want?" When looking back at it, I don't know how I managed to stay calm. I kept asking him what he wanted, and after I handed over the pills, he ran away as the security guard came down the aisle. The robber fired his gun as the guard gave chase outside, and the bullet hit a parked car. It was a frightening experience to have had that gun pointed at me. I could have been killed.

In Edmonton, I had an experience with a thief. I was counseling a patient at the pharmacy, and as I was concentrating on that, a thief came in and took my purse. It happened to be payday, so I had my paycheck envelope in there, as well as my ID, my watch, my credit cards, and other valuables. The thief used the cards to buy over $10,000 worth of furniture. She spent all that money in one day! She was later caught but only received a six-month sentence because she had a baby. I received no compensation, and it was a frustrating experience. In those days, I would often have to go to court to testify against people arrested for using fake prescriptions, but I had never felt so vulnerable in the courtroom as I did then.

Although I went through many difficulties like this, I poured all my life into the pharmacy, doing what my pharmacy alone could do. I came to know the faces and names of regular customers and what medications they took so that, when they came in, I could have everything prepared for them and give them exactly what they needed. I also made sure the pharmacy was always stocked with the medications they required. After 10 years, the community had come to know and trust Eagle Ridge Drugs, and the pharmacy entered a period of stability.

With the pharmacy now well established, I started to direct my energy toward helping to develop Korean pharmacists. Passing the qualification exam to obtain a pharmacist's license in BC is difficult and requires four to five years of preparation. To help them through this process, I took on pharmacy students from UBC and Ewha Womans University as student interns. By 2015, there was hardly a Korean pharmacist working in the area who had not gone through my pharmacy. I accepted anyone who wanted to intern. It was a lot of time spent on instructing and evaluating, but developing young pharmacists was rewarding work.

To be eligible to take the qualification exam, pharmacy students are required to intern for a period of one month if studying at UBC or three months in the cases of international students. The

internships could be completed only at a pharmacy designated by the College of Pharmacists, and my pharmacy was one, so my small pharmacy was always crowded. Even now, only about 1,000 out of 4,000 pharmacies in BC are certified by the College to administer the Covid vaccine. Of course, my pharmacy is one of them.

In particular, I worked hard to help create a foothold for pharmacists immigrating from Korea to settle in the Vancouver area. These pharmacists have a difficult time because they are required to complete a minimum number of volunteer hours but have trouble finding a pharmacy that will take them on. Because I am familiar with these barriers, I accept anyone relocating from Korea and help them get settled as if they were a member of my

With interns from Ewha Womans University's College of Pharmacy.

family. I feel it is the least I can do to repay the help I received when I first came to Canada.

Ewha Womans University pharmacy majors also came and took courses for credit. Although many Korean universities would have liked to send their students to study abroad like this, the cost of running such a program, which would require homestay arrangements, prevented them from doing so, but Ewha sent me students with a national scholarship. Being an Ewha graduate myself and now a practicing pharmacist in Canada, I was well positioned to help guide these students, and I was happy to do it. I found the Ewha students to be so intelligent and kind, they were like nieces to me.

I also hired a pharmacist to work with me. Her name was Kang Hye-kyung, and she had attended Kyunggi Girls' High School and Ewha Womans University, as I had, and she was nice and

With friends from Ewha Womans University College of Pharmacy, 1968.

sincere. I came to trust her enough to manage the pharmacy for extended periods of time, such as when I underwent my bronchial embolization in 2004. A few years later, she moved on to run her own pharmacy.

Pharmacist Kwak and his wife, who run a pharmacy next to Hanareum supermarket, also worked at my pharmacy, and Song Taek-hoon, a pharmacist who graduated from Seoul National University, started his own pharmacy after working at mine. I think of everybody I have worked with as family members, so if they need medication, I sell it to them for the invoice price. I provide good benefits and treat staff members like family, so there are many people who have worked for me for 10 or 20 years without leaving for anywhere else.

Then, in 2009, I purchased a building and opened a new pharmacy there, and my second son, Dennis, who had been working at Dr. Gill's clinic, opened his own clinic next to the pharmacy. When Dennis was still in school and studying psychology in another province, I asked him to come to Vancouver because there was a shortage of Korean-Canadian family doctors. He graciously took me up on my suggestion and went back to school to become a family doctor, and I am grateful that he is now serving the Korean community in Vancouver. Today, Dennis runs a clinic with six doctors. From 2010 until 2014, when I sold the first pharmacy, I managed two pharmacies. In 2014, I sold that first pharmacy, Eagle Ridge Drugs, to Ahn Hye-won, who used to work for me and is an Ewha Womans University graduate, and decided to operate only the other one, Oh Pharmacy.

Through my career as a pharmacist, I have been able to meet many people and gotten to know them as friends, and I love that the pharmacy can be a place to gather, for pharmacists, students, and people in the community. My pharmacy also serves as an office for the Vancouver Korean-Canadian Scholarship Foundation and the Rose of Sharon Foundation. In addition, the pharmacy is where I can provide medication to help sick people, learn and work hard to fulfill my dreams, and depend on as a source of financial stability. I would say that pharmacy is my life.

2. Hamilton, Toronto, and Winnipeg

Hamilton

I began my immigrant life in Hamilton, Canada, in February 1971. While attending graduate school at Ewha Womans University's College of Pharmacy and preparing to study abroad, I got married, on May 10, 1970. My husband, a religious studies major at Seoul National University, was accepted to a doctoral program at McMaster University, and at the completion of my studies at Ewha, I was accepted to graduate school at the University of Toronto, so we came to Canada together.

When we moved here, there weren't many Koreans in Canada. Near where we lived, there were only about 20 families, and Canadians didn't know much about Koreans, so there were many difficulties. But I could rely on help from my fellow Korean immigrants, who treated me like family, and I was able to quickly settle into my life in Canada.

Our journey to Canada began with a lot of love and support. More than 100 people -- family, friends, and professors -- came out to Kimpo International Airport to see us off when we left Korea on January 24, 1971. In celebration of our move, we made plans to make stopovers in Japan, where my brother-in-law was living; San Francisco, where my cousin Choi Soon-up and her husband, Kwak Do-chan, were living while he attended Stanford University; and Los Angeles, where one of my uncles lived. In

Japan, we did some sightseeing around Atami and drove up Mount Fuji, and I remember there was a lady selling tangerines and we bought a basket. I was three months pregnant at the time, and the tangerines were so delicious, I ate all of them by myself. But when we reached our destination, I threw them all up. In Los Angeles, I remember going to Disneyland and being pregnant and weighing about 45 kg and going around on all the rides, and my aunt was nervous about the baby. I was young, though, and didn't know how hard it was to be pregnant, but I was excited and happy about this time of a new beginning.

On the day we arrived in Toronto, Canada, February 2, there was a lot of snow, and the snowdrifts formed our first impression of Canada. We were so grateful that Pastor Lim Sung-won and his son-in-law, Oh Yeon-kyu, whom we knew from church in Korea, came out to greet us. They served us bean sprout soup for breakfast, which was very delicious, and nourished us for a good start to our first day in Canada. Then we went to McMaster University in Hamilton, which was about 60 km from Toronto. We continued to attend church after coming here and were welcomed by the members of the congregation, especially Mary Lister and Laura Sigurdson, who took great care of us. Mary Lister, an elementary school teacher, was a little older than my mother and looked after me like I was her daughter, and Laura Sigurdson would take us to her home after church each week and make us lunch. Thanks to them, I learned how to sew and was able to make maternity clothes that I could wear and make curtains and hang them, and in such ways, I was able to get by with their help. So, I was full of gratitude and worked hard as an active member of the church, singing with the choir, and my husband was in charge of Bible study group.

We had a lot of fun times with other Koreans and international students attending McMaster University. Yoo Jae-shin was a student in the Department of Religious Studies at McMaster. He would babysit for us and was like a member of our family. Kwon O-yul was a graduate of Seoul National University who was now completing his doctorate in economics at McMaster and his wife had graduated from Ewha Womans University's College of Pharmacy, so we became very close. We would meet again later living in Regina and then again in Vancouver. Our children were around the same age, so we would go on family trips together and share our parenting experiences. Their children would later go on

Eugene's first birthday, August 1, 1972.

Dennis is born at Severance Hospital, February 27, 1974.

to attend medical school in Kingston and become professors at the UBC Faculty of Medicine, and the younger one would perform back surgery on my husband. There was also Lee Seung-jae, a graduate student in mathematics who was married to a Chinese wife with whom I became very close friends, eating our meals together almost every day and raising our children together. They lived just down the hall from us, so when it was time to eat, we would bring side dishes and eat together, one day at our apartment, one day at theirs.

We both had our firstborns around the same time, so we became close as we helped each other through those first days of being new parents. At the time, I didn't know anything about how to take care of a baby, so I read books and followed the instructions, but feeding a baby and sterilizing a bottle were not easy like in the books. If the instructions said to soak the diapers in detergent overnight and then wash them, I would soak them overnight, wash them and dry them and this would go on for days on end. When our children were still newborns, we would greet each other asking, "Did you get any sleep last night?" It was an exhausting time, but we were going through it together, and we could understand and comfort each other. Lee Young-joon, Jung Hae-soo, and Lee Young-gu and their families were also close friends with whom we spent a lot of time during those years.

With all the challenges of being young, growing families, it was an arduous time for us in Hamilton, but we also had fun, gathering for get-togethers, going from home to home, eating

At my husband's PhD convocation, 1976.

meals together, putting our babies to bed next to each other, and talking late into the night. It was during this time that I first really experienced the great power of being together.

I also have fond memories of going foraging. In Canada, there are a lot of forests and open fields with gosari and chwinamul, so we could go out there and pick them to eat as side dishes. The government has since banned this practice, but back then we were free to fill bags as big as garbage bags. It was such a frequent activity, my toddler would say, "Mommy, chwinamul!" whenever we walked past any. In addition to the greens, I was able to buy ox tails, ribs, and other cuts of meat that Canadians didn't eat. It was 25 cents for an ox tail and 25 cents for a leg, and we ate like this every day. My mother had been worried we would not be able to eat properly as international students. I was grateful we could reduce our food expenses and eat healthy food. I also have delicious memories from after moving to Vancouver, of picking edible seaweed and toasting it to make gim, picking acorns and laying them out to dry before crushing them to make acorn jelly, and picking chestnuts and steaming them.

The Korean community has helped me adjust to immigrant life, but more than anything else, my husband and I relied on each other as newlyweds. Even though my husband was busy with his studies, we were able to attend prenatal classes together and looked forward to the birth of our child with excitement, and we spoke often about the kind of family we wanted to build. Thanks to those times, I think I was able to quickly overcome my fear of having a baby and the unfamiliarity of living in a foreign country. I will never forget how he stayed by my side during the birth of our child and cooked seaweed soup for me afterward.

The contractions were hard and fast, and I was in labor for four hours, feeling like I was going to die. In the delivery room, my husband was there to help me, reminding me to take deep breaths like we had learned in prenatal classes, and he recorded the sound of our child's heartbeat, but I was in so much pain I wasn't hearing anything. The births of our younger children, however, were easier. When Dennis was born, I was staying with my parents in Seoul, while my husband was in Japan to do research for his doctoral thesis. When I look back now, I think we were still learning to navigate our way through pregnancy and childbirth, but we were making progress a little bit at a time and becoming a stable family.

Between Eugene and Dennis, Daniel was born on March 1, 1973, but we had to part ways after only three months due to a congenital heart condition. I spent long nights holding my sick baby in the hospital. In the end, he went to heaven, and I was only able to bear the pain of that great loss because by my side was my husband, who was the one person who knew my pain because he was grieving just as I was, and we could cry together and comfort each other. It was not easy coming to this faraway foreign country as a student and giving birth and raising a baby, but those times of hardship also strengthened the love and trust my husband and I had with each other. I am so grateful that Dennis came to us the following year, like a gift from Daniel.

When we came to Canada, my plan was to start graduate studies right away, but I soon realized that with the pregnancy, the birth of our child, and my father's business undergoing some difficulties at the time it would be better to put that plan on hold. I decided that I would support my husband while he completed his studies before pursuing my own, so I started working as a pharmacy technician. I was very busy working at the pharmacy and raising a baby, and when I wasn't busy with those things, I was typing my husband's papers. Because the papers were about different religions, there was a lot of typing words in foreign languages, such as Sanskrit, which made the task very laborious. There were many times I would be up all night typing to make a deadline, but even after staying up all night I would go to work at the pharmacy in the morning.

Through all of this, my desire to study pharmacy never waned. I knew I needed to prepare for life after my husband's PhD. So, I traveled to Toronto by myself over his objections and enrolled as an undergraduate. Back then, Canada's pharmacy examining board did not recognize degrees from Korea, so I would have to complete two years of undergraduate study here before being eligible to sit for the pharmacist qualifying exam. I had just recently gotten my driver's license, and I remember making the harrowing one-hour drive to Toronto that day. The window was rolled down, but my nerves were so rattled and I was so focused on driving that I couldn't even roll it back up. After registering at the school, I didn't have the energy to make the drive back, so I left the car there and took the bus home. It had been a lot of work

With my family and my mother-in-law at Niagara Falls, 1976.

to enroll at the school, but compared to commuting to school every day afterwards, it was a breeze.

It was truly an eyewatering commute. Getting to class took two and a half hours. I would have to take public transit from our apartment to the bus terminal, travel by highway coach to Toronto, and then catch a transit bus to reach the campus. So, I would have to leave at four in the morning, which was not easy, but I gritted my teeth and was determined to complete my studies as quickly as possible. During classroom lectures, I was not able to understand English very well, so I would ask the students next to me if I could copy their notes and I would memorize them, and after I got home and the kids were in bed, I would go to the library and study. For my pharmacology and pharmacokinetic classes, I think I practically memorized the entire textbook.

Leaving my boys, who were three and one at the time, with a babysitter was not easy either. I don't know how many times I cried while dropping them off. Pastor Yoo's wife took care of the boys often and was of great help to me. Not only did she look after the kids, but she was also very attentive to my well-being. Being surrounded by such supportive people, I was able to complete my course requirements in one year. I passed the qualifying exam immediately thereafter and received my pharmacist's license in 1976, I was overjoyed! I was the only one among my classmates to pass, and only the third Korean ever. I think the achievement was even more rewarding because of all the tearful effort it took.

In the period leading up to the licensing exam, I was also completing an internship while studying and raising our two children, and I was being worn thin. It eventually reached the point where I was coughing up blood. The doctors were unable to determine the cause, so I just assumed it was pneumonia and took antibiotics and carried on.

On the day of the exam, I dropped off my husband and our boys at a motel near the testing site, and I remember becoming so overcome with emotion on the way to the exam that I began sobbing uncontrollably. I couldn't stop crying as I remembered the hardships I'd had to endure up to that point, all the studying, all the pressure, and all the fear about my health. If it weren't for my husband's support and my children's lovely smiles, I might not have been able to make it to the end.

What began with that overwhelming task of obtaining my pharmacist's license continued for the next 30 years. During that difficult period, my mind stayed strong, but my body could not. There were times I was coughing up so much blood I thought I was going to die right then and there. During my third pregnancy, I was hospitalized due to excessive blood loss, I couldn't play the flute anymore, and antibiotics weren't helping. I remember the terror I felt because there was so much blood.

Then, one day in 2004 during a visit to Korea, I was coughing up so much blood I couldn't breathe, so I was transported by ambulance to Samsung Hospital, where my friend Jong-hwa's husband was chief of surgery. I was able to get in right away to be examined and was diagnosed with bronchiectasis. Arteries in my bronchi had become inflamed and burst. I underwent an embolization procedure that stopped the bleeding, and at long last I could breathe free. It felt like being given new life, a precious one that I wished to live to the fullest.

Toronto

That is how I received my pharmacist's license in 1976, and after my husband obtained his PhD, he took a contract position at Miami University in the United States, while our children and I stayed in Toronto. I was now working full-time at a pharmacy, raising our children, and taking care of my mother-in-law who was

Family members from all over the world gathered in Vancouver, August 1997.

living with us. The pharmacy paid well, but it wasn't easy to come home after a long day of work and then take care of the kids. Still, when my mother-in-law asked for something to eat, I would make it right away and serve it to her.

For her birthday, we invited about 200 people from our church for a picnic feast at the park. We cooked her favorite dishes, while reminiscing about the food we used to eat as children, and I did my best to do everything according to her instruction. Because of all our time together, my mother-in-law felt the most comfortable at our house and liked staying with her youngest child the most out of all her children. At the time, my husband was one of seven brothers and sisters, his eldest brother having passed away at a relatively young age, and they all practiced great filial piety, as well as maintaining close relationships with each other, so whenever it was my mother-in-law's birthday, we all tried to gather for the occasion, whether it was in Korea, Japan, the United States, or Canada. I think I was naturally assimilated into this close-knit family and did my best to take care of my mother-in-law.

Winnipeg

We lived in Winnipeg from 1977 to 1978, the only time in my life when I didn't work. We were in a financial situation that didn't require me to have a job, and up to then I had been living such a hectic life of studying and working, it pained my heart to think about all that time I had to be away from my crying children. So even though I had obtained my Manitoba pharmacist's license, I took the bold step of putting my career on hold to focus on my children.

As I directed my energy into household work, most of my

In Banff, Alberta, July 1980.

attention became drawn to what we were eating. The Seventh-day Adventist Church encourages vegetarianism, and I decided we should adopt a vegetarian diet for its many health benefits. I put a lot of effort into preparing our meals, making my own tofu, from bean sprouts I grew at home, and it seemed I was practically living in the kitchen. But when I saw my children enjoying the food, I would forget about all the hard work and my mind would happily turn to what else I could feed them.

And the Korean church we attended in Winnipeg was a lot of fun. I played accompaniment on the piano, sang hymns, and went on trips with members of the congregation. We got along especially well with Kwon Byung-hyun, who was a church elder, and his wife, Kang Hwan-jo. Our children were similar in age, so we had a lot of fun on family outings together, taking them to swim at the pool on weekends and tobogganing and skiing in the winter. We went around so much together, the grandmother who lived with them would say we were raising our children throwing them in the water and throwing them in the snow. I thought children should run around and play so they could grow up healthy.

I also have fond memories of going on camping trips with our boys. We bought a red Buick Skylark hatchback with $3,000 we had saved up and used it to travel around in, and the boys would sleep in the back. My husband taught summer school in those days, and we would travel with him to where he was teaching. One summer, we lived in Moncton, New Brunswick. I remember we went out on a fishing boat off the Atlantic coast, and Eugene

Edmonton, Christmas, 1980.

was so excited when he reeled in a mackerel. The rest of us caught cod, and in Canada the heads are thrown away, but I love fish heads, so I brought them home instead of throwing them out. I filleted the fish and lay them out on the windowsill to dry, but the boys couldn't resist, and they and the birds ate them all.

When we went on holidays, I would pack food to take with us, so only rarely did we eat out, but I remember one time one of my husband's students worked at a crab fishery in Shediac and he got us a great deal on a box of crabs. We enjoyed them so much they were gone in no time. We didn't normally eat shellfish because our church considered it unclean as defined in the Book of Leviticus, but the crab we ate that day was heavenly. Perhaps God was worried that my love of this food would cause my cholesterol levels to go through the roof.

A funny thing happened around that time on a camping trip. The boys woke up in the night because they had to pee, but it was nighttime and the bathroom was far away, so I had them pee into an empty Coke bottle and we went back to sleep. In the morning,

I had forgotten about what happened and I drank it! We talked about this later and laughed. The memories of all our camping trips, from the Pacific to the Atlantic, splashing around in the water, sitting around the campfire, in the deep forest, surrounded by mountains, stargazing, talking, are all precious memories I will never forget. It was a time of enriching our boys' childhood, and we were so happy to be able to do it.

3. Edmonton, Regina, and Vancouver

Edmonton

Edmonton was our home for three years starting in 1979. My husband was teaching at the University of Alberta, and we lived in a very old house near the campus that the university rented us. One day, I was cooking beans in a pressure cooker and somehow the cooker exploded. Fortunately, nobody was hurt, but there were beans stuck all over the ceiling, and I have a funny and sad memory of standing on a chair picking beans off the ceiling in that old house.

There were many young families in the congregation at the church we were attending, and therefore lots of babies, and they were so beautiful. Perhaps it was due to seeing all these beautiful babies, but I became pregnant. I remember the good-natured teasing from the other congregants, because back then it was not common for women to have babies after turning 30 like I was. But having been through the experience of pregnancy before, I was able to appreciate this latest one as a time to be happy.

At the time, the oil industry in Alberta was booming and a lot of Koreans were moving to Edmonton to work as welders. Even with no previous experience, welders could earn $2,000 a week, so it was a time of economic prosperity, and there were a lot of homes being constructed to house the growing population. Around that time, many Koreans were building their own homes in an area called Mill Woods. I wanted to build a brand-new house like them and move out of our dilapidated one. Over my husband's objections, I went to city hall by myself and there I learned about Blue Quill, a new subdivision in the southwest part of the city, and a residential area being developed around there called Yellowbird Court. I bought a lot in Yellowbird where we could build our house. I didn't know anything about a building a house, though. Luckily, there was a carpenter named Yang Moonsam who went to our church, and I offered to hire him to be our contractor and we could build the house together. We started with nothing; I didn't even have a blueprint. Fortunately, I had a friend who had just completed construction on a beautiful house with high ceilings. I asked if I could borrow his blueprints, and based on those plans I designed my own house. From that point on, each step was a challenge. When we went to buy the building materials, I had to pay retail prices because I didn't have a builder's license. After building the frame of the house, we had no way of raising it, so I asked our fellow church members for their help and served them meals on the day of the frame raising.

Somehow, we managed to get the roof up but then had to stop for a month after Mr. Yang fell off a ladder, and then there was all the work of coordinating our schedule with the electrician's. We had to overcome countless obstacles, but we were finally able to complete the house after about a year. The joy was indescribable. We had started out wanting to build the biggest house in Edmonton. In the end, our house had two floors with a total area of 2,160 square feet (about 60 pyeong) and a basement and a cathedral ceiling like a church's. I still remember the excitement of the day we moved in. It was our new house built with our own sweat and tears, and it was the first house we ever owned. All the hardship we encountered during its construction seemed to fly away. Our youngest child, Jason, was born while we were living in this house, so it is a place with precious memories for us.

The joy, however, was short-lived, because almost immediately afterwards, the oil crash happened, and the mortgage rate soared to 20%. We were struggling to make the monthly payments. When my husband was offered a position at the University of Regina, we were unable to sell the house, so we agreed I would stay with the boys in Edmonton and he would move out there for the academic year.

I was working full-time at a pharmacy, and I would come home at night to find the children had made a mess of the house and I would have to clean up after them. I came home one night to find the boys asleep and pieces of banana all over the walls because they'd apparently been throwing bananas at each other. I was upset to find our new house like that, but it was boys having fun and I couldn't bring myself to scold them. It was fortunate that for two days a week Eugene, Dennis, and Jason, who wasn't even three months old at the time, could babysit themselves. Whenever I'm in town now, I try to stop by the house, where we raised rabbits in the backyard and buried jars in the ground to make delicious dongchimi.

In the fall of 1980, when our youngest son was three months old, my husband started working as a professor at the University of Regina. We were unable to sell the house, so I remained in Edmonton with the children until 1982 when we finally moved to Regina. We would live there for the next 10 years, during which time we experienced the famously harsh weather for which the area is known. Temperatures exceeded 40 degrees Celsius in the summer and dropped below minus 40 degrees in the winter. As well as for its cold winters, the province was also known for its prairies and wheat fields, and it was the largest producer of wheat in Canada. The land was so flat, with not a hill in sight, it was said if your dog got loose you could watch it run away for three days until it disappeared over the horizon.

After moving to Regina, I planted a large vegetable garden that included Korean peppers, which were a favorite of my family's. At Christmas, I would sow the seeds in small pots inside the house and by New Year's they would start to sprout into seedlings. Then, in June, when the weather was warm enough, I would plant them in the garden in the backyard and tend to them through July and August. After planting them outside, I would have to listen to the weather forecast every evening, because if there was going to be frost, I would have to cover the plantings with blankets, even if it was in the middle of the night, to prevent them from freezing. Additionally, watering the garden was not easy due to the large number of mosquitoes. Even with repellent, you would be swarmed by mosquitoes the size of water droplets. But when the first pepper was ready to be eaten, I would cut it into four pieces and we would eat them together and be happy. Growing vegetables was very hard work, but the joy of harvesting the tomatoes, peppers, cucumbers, squashes, lettuce, crown daisies, and other vegetables and sharing them with my family was so great that I would forget about the hard work and plant the seeds again in the winter. In Korea, I didn't even know how to cook rice, but after immigrating, I remembered all the foods I ate during my childhood, and I grew my own Korean peppers, and made my own meju, soy sauce, gochujang, doenjang, and kimchi to eat.

Our vegetable garden was also a source of joy for relatives who came to visit us. One year, my brother-in-law and his family visited us from Japan, and we made plans to go on a road trip to the Canadian Rockies in our van. I was packing the cooler with food for the trip, and I remember my brother-in-law went out into the garden and picked a bunch of peppers that he said were ready to eat. The way he enjoyed them with his meals throughout the trip remains a happy memory for me. My in-laws who lived in California also came to visit one summer. They drove up, 17 of them in a VW van -- it seemed like an endless line of people getting out of that little Volkswagen. The kids had a great time playing amongst themselves, running around in the fields, playing in the basement, and falling asleep exhausted at night. Even now, my nieces and nephews talk about how much fun they had at our house, but I remember being so upset at the time seeing them in their shorts, their legs covered in mosquito bites. I am grateful they have such happy memories from that summer, despite the hot weather and mosquitoes.

We lost our dog, Blacky, while traveling through the Rocky Mountains with my brother-in-law and his family from Japan. The hotel in Banff didn't allow dogs, so we tied her to a pole outside and when we came out in the morning she was gone and the boys were devastated. Even though I don't like dogs, I found that I had become attached to our dog, and when we were unable to find her no matter how hard we searched I too was in tears. In the end, we had no choice but to give up and return home without her. A few days later, I received a call from somebody in Moose Jaw saying we could come get our dog. A woman in Banff had found Blacky on the loose and following children around, which led her to think the dog's owner must be a child. She found contact information on a tag on Blacky's collar and put up a sign at a local restaurant asking if anybody driving to Regina could give her a ride. Fortunately, someone who could bring her as far as Moose Jaw responded. I was so grateful. As my husband and Eugene got in the car to drive over to get Blacky, I felt that Canadians were just as caring as Koreans. That woman could have just as easily walked past without paying any mind, but instead she thought of the children who must be missing their dog, and as a result our family experienced the warmth of the world.

If you look at photos from around this time, you'll notice the males in my family have similar hairstyles. That is because I cut their hair myself. One of the first things I bought after arriving in Canada was a hair clipper kit, which I used to cut my husband's hair and then later my children's hair. When I got my hair permed, my husband would do the rollers. At first, we did this to save money, but it must have become a habit, because even after we could afford to go to a salon, I continued to cut my family's hair. Once a month, they would come into the bathtub one by one, and I would use a large garbage bag with a hole cut in it for their heads to cover them. The boys began going to a salon for haircuts once they reached middle school, but the time when I would cut their hair remains a pleasant family memory. There was one time when my husband wrote an article for the Korean newspaper about immigrant life and he mentioned how in our family like in many in the immigrant community his wife was the family barber. Around that time, the South Korean government was cracking down on men with long hair. Police would apprehend men whose hair they deemed overly long and cut their hair against their will in a rough manner. One day, my husband went to a barber shop, and the barber, on seeing the haircut I had given him, exclaimed, "Oh my God, did you get your hair cut by the police?" It made for a funny story for the newspaper.

During our time in Regina, my husband and I would take our children camping whenever he was on summer break. On one occasion, one of my uncles came to visit, and we all went camping together. On the day of our return, we had made plans to meet friends for a picnic, so we went directly to the park, only to find no one was there. Sensing something was wrong, I made a call and was told there had been a flood and we should go home right away. I had heard in the past that the city experienced major floods every few decades but the costs of mitigating them were deemed to outweigh the benefits. I hurried home to find that all the food, belongings, and other items we kept in the basement were floating in water, and it all looked like a pile of garbage. The city did offer some compensation, but the cleanup was a monumental task that took months to complete. Once we had thoroughly cleaned every nook and cranny and everything was back to its previous state, I felt a sense of renewal. It was a special experience for the family, one that we will never forget.

I have many such weather-related memories from our life in Regina. I used to rent Korean drama videos and invite my friends over to watch them with me. One time, we were watching a drama called Love and Ambition and we laughed and cried together without realizing how late it was getting on a frigid winter night. When everybody got in their cars to go home, none of the engines would start because of the freezing cold. Everybody ended up having to take taxis home. While it was common knowledge that cars could freeze in such conditions, we were so engrossed in the drama we didn't even think about it. Also, American soap operas were very helpful to me in learning English. Shows like General Hospital and Another World were great for learning common everyday English expressions, which I would memorize and use in my own daily life. For me, watching dramas was a triple delight of

With my in-laws in California.

With my parents in Regina, around 1990.

entertainment, companionship, and learning.

Not only were we gathering to watch dramas together, but also

With my parents in Europe.

my husband was president of the Korean-Canadian Association in Regina, so we got to know the 20 or so Korean families there like they were family. We would get together even if there was no special reason to, and we had dinners at each other's houses so often we knew where all the spoons and chopsticks were kept. If there was some sort of event, like a big game on TV, we would have everybody over for a watch party, and cooking for 30 or 40 people by myself was no big deal. It was not a problem to roast a turkey in the oven and have all four burners going on the stove at once while I prepared the various dishes. After dinner, Kwon O-yul and my husband would tell jokes, and we all would take turns singing a song. It was so much fun, the evenings went by quickly.

Back then, immigrating to Canada for employment was relatively easy, so there was a steady flow of immigrants coming to the country. Many Korean families moved to Regina with the help of Park Wang-seo, who owned a chopstick factory and guided them through the immigration system and all the required

With my parents and my oldest son, Eugene, in China.

Celebrating my mother's 90th birthday, 2011.

paperwork. Sometimes there were as many as 10 families arriving in one year. For each new arrival, we held a welcome party, and there were a lot of such parties. All of our families would gather and prepare delicious food and share stories to try to help them with the adjustment. Due to the harsh conditions, however, many families left again within a year for other places, so there were a lot of farewell parties. Steven Yeun's family was among those who immigrated to Regina and lived there for about a year before moving to the Detroit area to be with relatives. It was with a heavy heart I watched each departure, each serving as a reminder of how difficult immigrant life was. But I also realized that joy is multiplied when people gather for a party, which sparked a desire to create a place where Koreans could come together.

My husband joined a few others in the community to create a Korean school where children could learn how to speak and write in Korean and gain exposure to their heritage and culture. The school also became where newly immigrated Korean children could meet and become friends. They could share their problems and find their identity as Koreans living in Canada together.

We not only raised our children together, but also gathered like family whenever one of us was hosting a guest visiting from Korea. When my friend Jong-hwa came to visit, she stayed for about a month, and it seemed like every day was a party. By the time she left, she was friends with everyone. When she first arrived, she was surprised at how cold it was and wondered why I lived there, but the warmth of our community made her forget about the cold weather and she returned to Korea with fond memories.

I've moved so much that I practically have a doctorate in moving. We moved three times while living in Hamilton and then we moved to Toronto and then to Winnipeg. Then we moved to Edmonton and then again to another house there, and then we moved to Regina, where we moved again, from one house to another. After so many moves, I had so much practice I could pack our whole home in one night, although every time it was an exhausting process, and I often wondered where we would ever settle down. But I was encouraged that our children were able to adapt so quickly to their new surroundings and grew up healthy and well-behaved.

Art class.

In 1990, my parents came to live with us in Regina. They went to English language school every day, never missing a class, even during the harsh winter months. They were as diligent as they were in their youth, and I admired their persistence and was inspired by it. When I was younger, my father was a business owner and my mom was devoted to church work, so they didn't spend much time together, but after they came to Canada, they did everything together as a couple. Seeing how close they became during that time made me wonder how my own life would be when I reached their age. My mother, on the other hand, saw that her beloved daughter whom she had raised with such care was struggling as an immigrant in a foreign country. She took pity on me and quietly assumed some of the household chores, putting my mind at ease and enabling me to concentrate on my work. My mother had been suffering from chronic back pain for most of her life, but when she started helping me around the house, her back actually improved. It was remarkable to see how, when she needed the strength to assist her daughter, she found a way, demonstrating the power of motherhood. And thanks to my mom's infinite support, I was driven to work harder at the pharmacy.

My desire to give my parents, who had given me everything throughout their entire lives, a better living environment was one more reason I wanted to move to Vancouver. During the drive from Regina to Vancouver, we stopped at a motel for the night and to save money I booked one room for all of us to share. I regret not booking two rooms because then my parents could have slept more comfortably. My father sometimes has trouble sleeping with the lights on, but I stayed up studying for my pharmacy exam and had the lights on all night. I still regret my thoughtlessness. Despite the inconvenience, my father, who has a gentle personality, never complained, and instead continued to support me. I want to strive to live a life that emulates his deep love and gentleness.

One thing that didn't change after moving to Vancouver was their daily routine. They would wake up early in the morning, rain or shine, and catch the number 160 bus for the one-hour ride to the English language center. After class, they would go to Stanley Park, where they would have their lunch and take a walk and make a stop in Chinatown for groceries before returning home. I was grateful to see them able to enjoy their old age together. I tried to travel with them whenever I could. In 1995, we went on an Alaskan cruise, and in 1996, we went on a tour through Europe. In 1998, we went on a Caribbean cruise with my uncle and his wife. We also traveled to China one year. I was trying to take them around, and the travel was so they could enjoy themselves, but it was also a time of rest and recuperation for me as I was so busy working, so I will always be grateful to them.

Vancouver

After moving to Vancouver in 1991, I was busy running my pharmacy for the next few years. Once things had settled down, I was able to entrust its daily operations to Kang Hye-kyung. That was also around the time when the Korean media and cultural center opened in Vancouver, so I enjoyed going there. First, I took an art class for housewives, and although I wasn't good at it, I learned a lot about how to draw. I went around and drew places and objects from life, making pictures of the totem poles at Burnaby Mountain Park, and I went to Burnaby Lake to paint a landscape with flowers. Being a beginner, I was told to draw what I saw, so that's what I did, but later I realized I could have imitated different styles too, but I didn't know that and just continued drawing in my own clunky way. One time around Halloween, I drew a picture of a pumpkin and my husband saw it and asked, "Is it garlic? A pumpkin?" There were moments like that. Nevertheless, it was great to be able to fully appreciate nature while drawing. I hadn't realized the world around me was made up of such beautiful colors. After I'd taken all the classes all the way up to the advanced levels, my drawing skills had improved significantly, and it was a rewarding experience.

Then I took a drama class where I wrote my own script and put on a play. The play was about the life of my older cousin, Wan-sook, who lives in the United States. I've always had a soft spot for Wan-sook, because she injured her back while hiking in college and has been struggling with chronic pain for most of her life as a result. Writing the script gave me a new understanding of her life and an opportunity to deeply empathize with her thoughts and feelings. It was a moving experience, and I gained a bigger appreciation for theater as a means of encountering other human lives on stage.

I also enrolled in a class on meditation. I had always been interested in meditation, so it was a natural choice. Waking up at dawn to meditate had become a crucial part of my daily routine, so I wanted to know more about it and take my practice to a deeper level. I was prepared to follow wherever the teacher could take me. The class at the cultural center allowed me to learn how to approach meditation more systematically, through discipline, mindfulness training, and kuksundo. When I learn anything like this, I immerse myself in it, and the learning process is exciting and fun for me.

Golf and swimming are two activities that I'm still learning and enjoying. I'm out at dawn to play golf even when the weather is bad, and I take every opportunity to go swimming. I also regularly practice balchigi and kuksundo, and I have noticed many health benefits. After exercising, I feel lighter in body and mind. I wonder if this is the secret to my health and happiness.

4. Welcoming Korean athletes

Whenever a Korean came to visit Canada, that person became a valued guest, no matter who they were, and we had many welcome parties for newly arrived immigrants from Korea. When we lived in Hamilton, Niagara Falls was nearby, so every time we were hosting a visitor from Korea, we would take them there, and this would occur several times a year.

One of the most memorable visits was when the Korean national basketball and volleyball teams came in 1976. About 15 members of the Korean national basketball team, including Park Chan-sook, who was known as the queen of Korean basketball, came to Canada to train and compete in the qualifying rounds of the Olympic games. The volleyball team arrived later in that same period.

It was very exciting to welcome these teams to Canada. There were only about 20 Korean families living in Hamilton at the time, so we were able to greet them like family. As they got off the plane, we waved Korean flags around to convey our heartfelt welcome. My husband was the interpreter for the team during their stay, so we were able to get to know them as we traveled around together. The local Korean community came together and cooked bulgogi and other Korean food, and the team often came to our home for meals and they would play with the children, making for some happy times. We were worried about the athletes getting an upset stomach, so we didn't make anything too spicy for them, but what's Korean food without kimchi and gochujang? So, we cooked with kimchi and gochujang and served them with care, and seeing how much they enjoyed the food was such a joy! We felt like they were our own younger siblings, and it was so heartwarming and pleasant to see.

At the time, our children were two and five years old. When Park Chan-sook went around holding them in her arms, they didn't know she was a star athlete, they just sensed that she was friendly, and would happily stay tucked in her arms. We greeted and supported each other so warmly that it was hard to believe that we could become so close in the space of just a few days. We attended every game to cheer the team on, and at one of the games my younger son, Dennis, was crying and I was carrying him outside when a photographer captured the moment. The picture appeared in the newspaper with the caption, "Not everybody was happy."

When the time came for the team to return to Korea, we were so sad to say goodbye that we hugged each other in tears. It had been just a few short years since we'd left Korea, and it had been such an emotional experience to meet the Korean national team in a foreign country. Park Chan-sook also expressed her gratitude, saying she'd never received such hospitality anywhere else in the world, and later visited my parents in Korea.

I have had many experiences in Canada that made me feel patriotic, much like my encounter with the Korean national team.

With Cuban compatriots, 2002.

With fellow learners of samulnori.

Among the more memorable moments were those times I would sing the Korean national anthem as a representative of Korea at taekwondo competitions in Canada. There were times when I missed the first note and felt embarrassed, but representing Korea made my heart swell with pride. I had not felt so patriotic in Korea as I did after moving to Canada.

5. Visit to Cuba

In April 2002, I traveled to Cuba for about a week on a cultural mission to visit Cubans of Korean ancestry. I went with a delegation of 10 people, which included Lee Il-sung, Kim In-soon, Yoo Mi-ok, and Kim Jung-ja, all from the Vancouver area. During our visit as cultural ambassadors, we played traditional folk games, performed mask dances, and taught Korean songs. We also distributed gifts such as hanboks, ink sticks, matches, and ballpoint pens. The Koreans we met during our trip were descendants of immigrants who had arrived several generations ago, but they still carried pride in their heritage and a longing for their homeland. Their presence left a lasting impression in my heart.

Around that time, I was learning how to play samulnori from Han Chang-hyun in Vancouver. I had begun taking lessons only out of a desire to learn, but as my skills developed, I had the opportunity to perform at various Korean community events, such as parades and mask dance performances, and in this way help introduce Korean culture to Canada, so I was enjoying the class. Among those who were learning along with me in that class was Lee Il-sung.

Mr. Lee had a great love of Cuba and often traveled there as a missionary. So even though it was a difficult time to visit the country, I was able to go there thanks to him. Our itinerary included travel through various cities including Havana, Matanzas, and Aldelas, but the people living there did not have freedom of travel within their own country, so we had to go to each city unaccompanied by a guide.

Tragically, there was a plane crash in Cuba during our visit. Upon reading about it in the newspaper, my husband became distressed when he couldn't get in contact with me. The news of the crash brought a dark cloud over our stay that put all of us on edge.

In Cuba, there is a painful history of Koreans and the henequen industry. Korean emigrants had gone there in search of a better life, but their hopes turned to despair due to the deception of slave traders and Japanese brokers who sought to profit from the weak people of a powerless country. At that time, there was a racial hierarchy in Cuba, and Korean slaves were treated like livestock, ranking seventh, compared to Black slaves who ranked sixth. Many people died from the grueling labor of harvesting henequen from dawn to late at night in the extreme heat. Others were cut by thorns, resulting in wounds on their arms and legs that would become infected or lead to blindness. Those who were caught trying to escape were often beaten to death.

Despite such hard conditions, however, Koreans persevered with their characteristic diligence and patience. While enduring difficult labor, they also raised funds for the Korean provisional government and formed Korean associations to come together to find ways to overcome the challenges, while comforting each other to keep their spirits high. As we learned about this history during our visit at a museum, my heart welled up. There were also Koreans who risked their lives to escape and inform King Gojong about the horrors of Korean slavery, and their courage also deeply moved me.

Efforts to repatriate Koreans were thwarted by Japanese interference, and in the whirlwind of history, Koreans lived in Cuba for six generations without ever returning to their homeland. Nowadays, many Cubans of Korean descent have intermarried with Cubans and assimilated, making it difficult to distinguish between Cuban and Korean. Yet they still hold affection for their Korean heritage and pride in their identity. As I watched them sing Arirang and struggle to speak what little Korean they could remember, I felt a strong sense of togetherness and unity that is difficult to articulate.

It was amazing to see that these people were continuing to gather and live as Koreans even after so many years, and it pained me to know that they couldn't travel to see Korea although they might have wanted to and were thus made to live disconnected from the land of their ancestors. I hope that Koreans living in various parts of the world, not just in Korea, can remember this history and help them. I also think the Korean government should think about providing support for these people.

Chapter 3 :

Faith and
meditation

1. Seventh-day Adventist Church

My faith is rooted in Christianity. My belief in God, who resides in the deepest depths of my being, serves as the driving force and center of my life. Because I have faith that God is always with me, through both joyful and difficult times, I can live with a grateful heart, regardless of the circumstances. Moreover, I believe that I should let the boundless love and grace that God has given me spill over to my neighbors.

This is something I learned from my parents. Growing up, I saw my parents center their lives on the church and care about their neighbors so it was only natural I would do the same. My parents had both been born and raised in a Christian family. My paternal grandfather was a church elder, and my maternal grandfather, a graduate of Kyunggi High School and a descendant of the royal family, was an early leader of the Korean Seventh-day Adventist Church, serving as an interpreter for missionaries and establishing churches and fellowship centers before being martyred during the Japanese occupation.

The Christian education I received at church was the single greatest influence on my life when I was growing up, and living according to the words of the Bible was the most important goal in my life. As I read the Bible and learned about the life of Jesus, my faith grew, and through various volunteer activities with the church, I learned how to put Christian teachings into practice.

God's word is always good and powerful, so it was inevitable that learning and practicing His word would captivate my life and soul. A spiritually significant experience was when I felt an encounter with God.

It was when I was living in Edmonton. I was still an active member of the Seventh-day Adventist Church and living a very church-centerd life, when I had a very bad experience with the leader of the church I was attending. I remember being very confused when he told me, "You cannot serve your husband and the church at the same time, so you will have to decide whether to choose your husband or the church." Coming from the church I had served and whose teachings I had believed all my life, this

Sedona.

Sedona.

With fellow practitioners in Sedona.

wasn't something I could just ignore, So I prayed, "God, what should I do?" And for the next month, I barely ate or drank anything as I sought God's guidance.

At that time, I used to occasionally accompany my husband to Quaker meetings. During these meetings, which would typically last an hour, we would sit in a circle facing each other and remain silent and if someone felt moved to speak they would share their message and then the meeting would return to silence. At one of these meetings, I was meditating and had an incredible experience that is hard to describe. Suddenly, an inexplicable joy bubbled up in the center of my chest like soap bubbles, and I felt so happy, so overwhelmed with happiness, it was truly fantastic. It felt like heaven. Everything was bathed in a pure white light and a divine sound seemed to fill the universe. I felt incredibly light and joyful, and my body felt no pain or suffering.

After that experience, I began waking up at dawn every day to meditate and I didn't want to leave that state of mind, so I would meditate for more than five hours a day. Then as I went to work I would see people on the road and I would want to hug them all. I saw them as God's children, and everything was beautiful, whether it was flowers or whatever it was. I realized, "Ah, this is God's love!" I realized I had been looking at God, who is great and merciful, through an overly narrow lens. Once I understood that the church was not the only truth, I was able to see a wider world, and my mind became more free. I realized that what the church leader had told me was wrong because it came from a blind faith in God. It was a turning point for me, moving from a childlike faith that blindly followed the church leader's words as God's word to a mature faith as a Christian.

Looking back, I think that's when I met God. I was in a very difficult place in my life, and I reached out to God for answers, for a deeply meaningful encounter, and He reached out to me. Or perhaps He had always been in my heart and with me all along, there for me when I needed Him.

2. Meditation

The experience of meeting God that day was so good, I meditated diligently with the thought of wanting to experience it again. I traveled all over the world to find a good meditation teacher to learn from, and I also participated in rigorous training programs. Although I was busy running a pharmacy, the time for meditation was always a priority.

After starting with kuksundo, dahnhak, and mindfulness training, I was able to further deepen my understanding of meditation through temple stays and Vipassana. I studied at dahnhak centers in Vancouver and Sedona, Arizona. For mindfulness training, I visited mindfulness centers in Vancouver, Gyeryongsan in South Korea, and Los Angeles. I traveled to Haenam and other temples all over South Korea for temple stays. And to learn about Vipassana meditation, I studied at centers in Vancouver and the Rocky Mountains and at the Bodhi Tree Vipassana Center in Gwacheon, South Korea.

In the very beginning, I started meditation training at a dahnhak center. Founded by Lee Seung-hun, dahnhak aims to bring body and mind into a harmonious state through ki training, and I became a practitioner at a center in North Vancouver in 2002. There, I practiced by completing 108 bows while reciting incantations and performing body exercises. As I learned more about it, I became curious about Sedona, where the best place in the world for ki is said to be located and where there was a dahnak training center. To be able to train there, however, one had to meet certain requirements, as it was a place that trained instructors. So, I worked harder to meet the requirements. Eventually, the work paid off, and I was able to visit Sedona for training.

I enrolled in a two-week meditation program, which required waking up at dawn to recite mantras and perform 108 bows. I did this from 4 am to 9 am, and then attended lectures, observed instructors, and tried my best to do the body exercises. After two weeks, I had a conversation with my teachers. Although I was inexperienced and had many shortcomings, they seemed to recognize my pure passion and only talked about what I did well. Their compliments encouraged me to believe I could achieve an even deeper level of practice. I also felt a sense of regret that the program was so short. As a result, I decided to continue with a three-week training program and even become an instructor. Because of my nature to pursue things until the end, I worked hard during my time at the dahnhak center. By the end of my training, I realized that physical and mental training are connected, and I developed a habit of always starting my meditation practice with exercises.

During my stay at the center, my roommate was a university professor from California, who asked if I wanted to try past life regression, and I agreed out of curiosity. Following my roommate's instructions, I closed my eyes and envisioned my past life, and

I saw an endless stairway leading into darkness. As I descended the stairs, a figure appeared at the bottom. It was a monk walking barefoot in an empty field. He arrived at a hut where various tin bowls were placed, and he began to do zazen. Then he began levitating into the air, and I realized he was a monk who had attained enlightenment. My roommate said that monk who died while doing zazen was me in a previous life, and before that I was a big man who lived in Finland and heroically fought against attacking beasts to save the villagers. And in a previous life before that, I was a king. I don't believe in past lives, but I think the stories can provide courage and confidence for living in the present. After I woke up, the leader of the dahnhak center told me that if I hadn't come back up the stairs I descended, my life would have been in danger, so my roommate and I were sternly scolded. Nonetheless, it was a very strange and fascinating experience for me.

Afterwards, there was a time when a director of a meditation center, Master Woo, came to stay at our house for a few days, and through that friendship I began visiting the center to learn to meditate. I also traveled to Gyeryongsan to train for three weeks. In mindfulness training, you spend 24 hours focusing on your inner self, reflecting on your life from birth to present. The goal of this deep introspection on your inner self is to know exactly who you are and to have a peace of mind that cannot be shaken in any situation. You imagine killing your present self and to remember your life in the past. You recall your life as far back as you can remember until now, you attend your own funeral, and you ascend to heaven to look down on where you lived. Through this process, you throw away all feelings of guilt and regret, and thus liberate yourself. I have found this practice has helped me to learn more about how and why we meditate, which has helped me to deepen my meditation practice.

I have also been able to practice meditation through temple stays in areas of South Korea where the ki is good, the air is clean, and the forests are dense. When I visit the country, I make sure to set aside a week or so to do a temple stay, no matter how busy the schedule is. That is how important meditation is in my life. The temples are in the mountains, so naturally a part of any visit is to go for walks. It is so nice to walk in the mountains surrounded by beautiful forest that it feels like meditation. I would spend hours on these walks, and there have been some close calls. During a visit in Haenam, I was up at dawn to go for a light hike up a mountain, but got caught in a downpour. In a hurry to get back, I slipped on a wet boulder while descending and almost fell to my death.

Despite the danger, I went out again at dawn the next day in search of a hermitage deep in the mountains. I was told it would be a five-hour round trip, but I set off without hesitation with a light heart, thinking I would be back before breakfast. As I started walking on the path at dawn, the whole world was quiet and I could focus on every step. It was wonderfully meditative, but I was also afraid a wild animal might come out in the dark. At that moment I remembered the teachings of Wonhyo and pushed away my fear, and continued walking. After about two hours, when I thought I might be close to my destination, I came to a staircase. Although I couldn't see where it ended, I began going up the stairs and didn't stop. As I was going up, a monk was coming down, and I asked him how far I was from the hermitage, and he said it was just around the corner, so I pressed on. Reaching the top of the stairs, I saw the hermitage in the distance and ran towards it with joy. However, there was no one there, and it was deserted. The head monk I went there to meet was the one I met on the stairs earlier. Although I was disappointed, the hermitage's serene setting against the morning sky was more beautiful than any work of art. The experience of meditating alone at the hermitage was a special moment I would never forget.

Vipassana, which means to see things as they really are, is

Camino de Santiago, April 2018.

an ancient meditation technique whose most important aim is to be awake to every moment. In doing so, it allows you to let go of the ego and gain wisdom through true perception. The practitioner engages in mindfulness of breathing to reach a state of enlightenment. At a Marriott located in the Canadian Rockies, I meditated around the clock. At first, I ate only breakfast and lunch, and then for the last week, I fasted and concentrated only on my breathing, meditating in silence. My body empty, my thoughts focused only on breathing, my mind was clear. After two weeks of meditation, I was able to maintain this clear state of mind for longer periods of time, and I could see I was in a peaceful state,

Camino de Santiago, April 2018.

free from the bondage of the mind.

Since that time, I have continued to follow the practice of clarifying the mind through fasting. I fasted and meditated for the first week of this past January. Even after not eating for a week, because my mind had been emptied of all thoughts of food, I did not think about it. After the week was over, when it was time to start eating again, I felt a rush of hunger. During my fast, I was cooking tteokguk for my guests to have on New Year's Day, but didn't feel any appetite even with food right in front of me. Then when it was time to break the fast, I was preparing a meal with mukguk and I was eager to eat again. I realized then how great the power of the human mind is.

While searching for a place to practice Vipassana in Korea, I learned about the Bodhi Tree Vipassana Center in Gwacheon, near Seoul. The monk I met there, Buddhalagita, had been a dancer in New York City before discovering meditation and traveling to Myanmar to become a monk. Vipassana emphasizes fasting for a clear mind, and Buddhagalita meditated every day eating only one meal a day. The center was open to anyone who wanted to practice meditation at any time, and it operated on a donation-based system in which one could contribute what they could afford. Although the facilities were a bit outdated and there were some inconveniences, such as having to do laundry by hand, I found that Vipassana was the most suitable for me. Before I learned about this place, I used to travel around the country, doing temple stays and the like, but now I only come to the Bodhi Tree. Buddhalagita's book has also had a positive impact on me, and our conversations have helped me to deepen my understanding of meditation.

Even now I meditate every day at dawn. I don't think it's important to choose a specific technique, but rather to apply the strengths of each method and practice them consistently. Meditation is being present and mindful at every moment of the day, whatever you're doing. I believe that the purpose of my existence in this world is to purify and improve my soul. When looking back at the end of my life, I want to be a good person who has contributed to making lives better for people, and I am confident that diligently cultivating my soul through meditation will help me achieve my goals. I also believe that meditating creates a virtuous cycle that improves the health of both body and mind. This is why I meditate.

When I meditate, I pray, "Lord Jesus Christ have mercy on me," instead of reciting a Buddhist mantra. This is because I have come to realize that, in my own life, prayer and meditation are intertwined. I also believe that resolving many religious conflicts depends on recognizing that the fundamental essence that flows through all religions is the same, rather than being bound by the formality of religious practices. My friends with whom I attended church as a child may say that I have changed, but we are of the same mind because we know we encounter religion in the deepest parts of our souls.

In January 2018, I accompanied my husband on a trip to Myanmar, inspired by the fact that Buddhalagita had gone there to become a monk. As a Buddhist country, Myanmar has many temples, so I toured through many of them with my travel companions and visited several on my own. I had gone to Myanmar with high expectations, but I was very disappointed by what I saw. The temples were extravagantly decorated with gold, and visitors were asked to give offerings so that they may be reborn in paradise. I saw that the poor were being made poorer by their religion. While this is a problem in other countries, it seemed worse in Myanmar. I couldn't help but be saddened when I realized that religion was exacerbating poverty in Myanmar, with people on one side of a narrow alley living like beggars and the other side living like royalty. Visiting the temples prompted me to reflect on the proper role of religion, and I prayed that Buddhism in Myanmar could be reinvigorated both religiously and socially to help the poor. I believe religion should be for making people's lives free and peaceful.

One of my favorite memories of traveling for meditation was my trip to Spain in April 2018 to walk the Camino de Santiago to the Cathedral of Santiago de Compostela. I spent a week walking from Portomarin to Santiago de Compostela via Pala de Rei and Ribadiso de Baixo with Mr. and Mrs. Ko Young-kyu, whom I'd met as fellow practitioners of Korean Zen. The route was 130 km long, and we walked about 30 km each day. I didn't realize how hard it was going to be, and embarked on the pilgrimage without any fear, like a day-old puppy. I thought that if worse came to worst I could take a taxi. I went one step at a time, making sure I'd packed comfortable shoes and any medications that might be needed, and I hired a transport service that would pick up my luggage at each hostel and deliver it to the next one.

On the first day, I was able to keep up with the group, but I could sense that a couple I was with who were in their 40s was having to slow down to stay with me, so I told them to go ahead and went along at my own pace. Even though I was on my own, it was fun to walk along the path, sometimes through forests, sometimes through open fields, and there were signs indicating the way. Sometimes it was difficult going up the hilly terrain, and I got lost at times, but meeting and chatting with the other travelers on the road made me forget about the hardships. After I walked 28 km on the first day, my confidence grew.

On the second day, I increased my pace and caught up with a group of fellow travelers as they rested at a stop. They invited me to join them for something to eat and some time to relax at a restaurant. I knew, however, that if I stopped then it would be hard to get started again, so I apologized, took a breath, and kept walking. I remembered such moments in my life's journey, when during a period of struggle when I thought I would collapse I would have to fight the urge to let up. As if to comfort my weary soul after a long, hard day, the sunset lingered on the red dirt road. I felt grateful that my mind and body had been strengthened by enduring those moments.

I arrived at the hostel safely, but when I got there, I saw that my friends were suffering from blisters on their feet. This is where the medications I had brought became useful. I set up a small pharmacy and provided treatment. I got so used to walking that if I started off early in the morning, I could reach the next hostel by two or three in the afternoon. On the road, it was nice to form friendships with the other travelers, and at the end of the day it was a great pleasure to get in the water and relax my tired muscles. The highlight was arriving at Santiago de Compostela on the final day and having my pilgrim's passport stamped with the compostela, the certification of accomplishment given to pilgrims upon completing the Camino de Santiago. I was so excited to receive the stamp that I forgot about all the hard work and enjoyed the final dinner with a happy heart. From Spain, we traveled to Portugal and went around in a rented car. The seafood we had in Portugal was so delicious! Perhaps the joy of having completed the pilgrim's way made it twice as delicious.

The pilgrimage route, the path that James, a disciple of Jesus, walked from Jerusalem to spread the Gospel, is so deeply engraved with history and culture that it was designated as a UNESCO World Heritage Site in 1993. Although my journey began with a vague desire to walk along the path where the Gospel was preached, as I walked on this path that embodies the stories of pilgrims from all over the world, I could feel the venerable energy of all those who had walked before me. Every step felt like a moment of meditation, as I walked with a single-minded focus, awakening myself to each moment. This trip to Spain, where I was able to feel the steps of Jesus through meditation, remains a very precious memory to me.

Chapter 4 :

Home life

1. Marriage

My husband, Professor Oh Kang-nam, is an intelligent and wise man who has read a lot of books and helps me realize the wisdom of life. He has a talent for talking about difficult topics in an easy and entertaining way, so even just laughing and talking with him puts my mind at ease and helps me organize my thoughts. We have been together for over 50 years, and throughout the years, I have felt I should support him so that he can be successful and have a good influence on others.

We first met when I was in college and a member of a student association for Seventh-day Adventists in Seoul. I was the vice

Our wedding at Jongro Ceremonial Hall with families and relatives, May 10, 1970.

president and he was the advisor, so we got to know each other naturally through our student council activities and many conversations about faith. Also, his mother and my maternal grandmother knew each other, and his sister-in-law was friends with my uncle and aunt from their time living in Japan, so our families knew each other. When my husband was a teacher at Sahmyook Middle and High School, an aunt on my mother's side was also teaching there and thought highly of him, and she recommended him to my family as a possible marriage partner.

We were engaged on August 14, 1969, and got married on May 10 of the following year, so we had a long engagement. I have many fond memories of our dates. On weekends, we would go hiking together, to Baekundae, Bukhansan, and Dobongsan, and we traveled all over with friends. My husband read a lot of books, so there was an endless number of things to talk about, and he also made me laugh a lot, so when we were together, we had long conversations without noticing the passage of time. He would also be invited to gatherings with my friends, where he would tell funny stories, and my friends would tell me they thought he was cool and that would make feel like I was cool, too.

Our marriage received the blessings of our families and the church. Both my husband and I were conscientious students who listened to our elders, worked hard for the church, and excelled academically, so we were both raised with a lot of love, and many believed our meeting was predestined. We were able to start our marriage with lots of affectionate attention and congratulations from those who were happy to see us marrying a good man and a good woman.

Once we were married, I was able to observe my husband more closely and appreciate his remarkable intelligence. He possessed an excellent memory, and I naturally came to admire him when I would see him always reading. It would make me happy when he would share with me what he was reading and tell me his thoughts. In this way, my husband taught me, a science student, the joys of humanistic reasoning and led me to think deeply about the meaning of human life. All our conversations came naturally during our daily lives. During this time, my perspective on the world broadened, and I was able to imagine the future we would create together.

I was blindly immersed in the teachings of the church, but my husband, a scholar of religion, thought in a different way. He emphasized that one should become a believer of profound religion, not a surface-level religion. He awakened me to the importance of not being bound by formalities such as doctrines and dogmas, to break free from my preconceived notions and thus attain enlightenment. Even while he continued to attend church with me following our marriage, he would work hard to change my fixed ideas about the church. Sometimes, when I was sleeping, I would hear him talking fervently next to me, and when I asked him what he was doing, he said he was teaching true religion to my subconscious. Thanks to his efforts, I was able to free myself from the rigid teachings of the church. I no longer felt guilty for not attending church every week or eating foods that were forbidden by the church. I am truly grateful for this, but the important thing I learned from my husband was to open my eyes spiritually and experience the reality of God through a shift in consciousness.

As I learned more about my husband's studies in comparative religions, I was struck by his extraordinary insights and became convinced that he could make a positive impact on the world. So I did everything in my power to ensure that he could focus on his studies without worrying about money or parenting the children. While other international students had to work part-time to get by, I took charge of the family finances so that he wouldn't have to work and instead be able to devote himself to completing his studies. My husband's yearly stipend was $3,600. I would go to the supermarket and manage to buy a cart full of groceries for just $15. Also, I was able to work part-time and supplement our income that way. It wasn't easy to balance work and raising young children, but it was for a dream that my husband and I shared, and I was willing to do whatever it took to make it a reality.

My husband had a great passion for research, which led him to attend conferences and travel extensively throughout Europe, China, Japan, and Southeast Asia for the purpose of conducting research. Although it was challenging at times due to his extended absences, I drew upon all my strength because I believed it was my mission to support his research. And the children were still young, and each day was so busy, the time would pass quickly without any feelings of loneliness.

In 1986, my husband set off on a six-month visit to India and Tibet among other destinations. But he had to cut the trip short after just one month because he was bitten by a dog in India and had difficulty finding a rabies vaccine locally. It was a stressful time, and my heart was filled with anxiety. Even now, just thinking about it makes me lightheaded.

Despite returning home in a state of high anxiety, my husband had not forgotten to bring me back a gift, a piece of jade jewelry. He'd purchased the item based on the advice of a guru he met in India who told him that if I ever passed away and he wished to remarry but I didn't want him to, he could let me keep the cat eye jewelry. So, while he hadn't bought the gift for romantic reasons, I appreciated that even during a life-or-death emergency, he had been thinking of me.

The heavens must have known how much I wanted to support my husband, and his career took off like a sailboat in a gentle wind. Shortly after receiving his PhD, he was offered a teaching position at a university and later joined the faculty at the University of Regina. Since I was in charge of running the household, he had more time to devote to his research and write several books. As his profile rose and he became more respected, I felt rewarded and happy knowing that all our hard work was paying off. During his travels, a guru he met in India told him that he was here in this life only to enjoy it. I can't help but feel that my dedication and hard work to support my husband is reflected in those words.

During a lecture, my husband once made a humorous remark that in our household I was responsible for the small things, such as managing the family finances, raising our children, and buying our houses, while he focused on the big things, such as promoting world peace, but now with me attending international peace conferences he joked that even the big things were being taken away from him. While talking about fear in a recent interview with SBS Biz, he shared another humorous anecdote. He recalled how he worried about finding a job as a professor after completing his doctorate, but he took comfort in the fact that I was working as a pharmacist at the time, joking that he could always sweep the floor at my pharmacy. I found his humor endearing, and felt his comments reflected his affection and trust in me.

My husband's sense of humor shines when he delivers lectures. He has a knack for making people laugh even when he is discussing serious and difficult topics. I am impressed by how he uses wit strategically to change people's perspectives. He often tests his jokes on me before delivering them to a wider audience, and we have a lot of fun together laughing. It's a privilege to hear his jokes before anyone else and it brings us closer.

Of course, there are times when conflicts arise due to our different personalities. For instance, when I cook, I tend to make a lot of food because I feel better when there are leftovers. When I'm preparing a meal for guests, I want them to be able to eat as much as they want, so I make plenty. My husband, however, insists that I should make only enough for one meal so that there are no leftovers, and we always end up quarreling about that. In addition, I've received a lot of criticism for my tendency to take charge and make things happen instead of sitting still. When we were building our house in Edmonton, my husband thought it was reckless of me to take on something so challenging by myself, and he objected to the fact that I kept the children too busy with sports activities and music lessons. Our sleeping habits are also different. He writes late into the night and goes to bed around two in the morning, while I am just about to wake up and start the day, so our schedules are opposite. Just as night

을 염려하시는 어머님께 저의 생각이 어머님의 생각과 어느 면에서는 달라도 전혀 염려하실 바가 없다는 것을 끝내 확신시켜 드리지 못한 것 같기 때문입니다. 하나님께서 어머님의 마음을 위로하시고 아들에 대한 어머님의 크신 사랑에 후히 보답해 주실 것만 바랄 뿐입니다.

무엇보다도 제 머리에, 가슴에, 팔에 변하지 않는 힘을 넣어 준 이, 인생길에 반려자로서 세 아들을 같이 키우는 동역자로서만이 아니라 구도의 길에 더 바랄 수 없이 아름다운 '길벗'으로 끊임없는 슬기와 용기의 원천이 되어 주는 이, 전에는 우리가 가는 목적지의 번지수가 다를 것이라 각오하고 있었는데 이제 그것이 천국이든 지옥이든 도솔천이든 'nowhere'이든 분명 같은 곳이 될 것이라고 생각하면……

아, 그대에게 복이 있으라!

1981년, 캐나다 리자이나 대학 한 모퉁이에서

오 강 남

In the introduction of my husband's book.

and day are opposites, however, so are yin and yang, and the world needs both for harmony. Because we have these different tendencies, we naturally make up for what the other lacks and create harmony.

Despite our different personalities, my husband and I have been able to maintain a peaceful marriage for a long time, and I attribute this to our "airy marriage." In an airy marriage, there is room for the wind to blow between two people, but it also means air travel is required. Over the years, we have spent significant time apart. We got married in 1970, and a few years later, from November 1973 to May 1974, my husband went to Japan to conduct research while I stayed with my parents in South Korea. From September 1976 to June 1977, he was in Ohio while the rest of us lived in Toronto with my mother-in-law. From 1980 to 1981, he was teaching in Regina while I stayed with the children in Edmonton. From 1991, when we moved to Vancouver, until his retirement in 2006, we lived apart for three months in the fall semester and three months in the spring semester, while he taught at the University of Regina. During each vacation, I would pack three months' worth of side dishes for him to take back with him to Regina. Since his retirement, he has been living for several months out of the year in Korea. Although it was not intentional, the times of being apart created space in our marriage where we could breathe. As the saying goes, we missed each other when we were apart and withered away when we were together, but I think we are doing so well today, despite our many differences, because we had that space.

If I had to choose the happiest time I've spent with my husband, I would say it was during our family trips. Both of us love to travel, so in the summers we would take our children on long road trips and camp along the way. I would pack a cooler with Korean food, and we would eat in the car. To keep the boys entertained, we would tell old stories and play road-trip games, and upon reaching our campsite, we would start a campfire as the sun went down. I have many happy memories of grilling meat and afterwards roasting marshmallows, corn on the cob, and potatoes while the boys ran around playing. In the morning, while the children slept in the car, we would set off for our next destination. If we were by the ocean, we would go deep-sea fishing, and bring our catch home, clean the fish, and lay the fillets out to dry, only to have them all gobbled up by my impatient children. We would sit around the fire, listening to the crackling of the wood under the starry night sky, talking. My husband would listen to me and my children for a long time, as if to make up for the time we were apart. I think the stories we shared during those times continue to provide us wisdom and comfort in our lives to today.

A letter from my husband to me

1:40 pm, Friday, March 20, 1981

Honey!

Thank you for your letter yesterday. When I read that you

thought your whole body was melting with love, I felt like my body was melting, too. If we both melt away like this, who will raise the children? But I'm sure that not everything would melt away like when a snowman melts, but rather, after everything else in us is gone, there would remain our pure and unadulterated incarnation of love.

My beloved, I received your call last night. I'm glad to hear all is well. Please take good care of yourself. As I mentioned in today's lecture at school, things are not independent but interdependent. Everything is related to each other. Your being healthy, happy, fresh, beautiful, and kind is not just your own business, but it is directly related to the peace and happiness of all of us. Taking care of yourself is taking care of us...

It's already the weekend again. It's both good and sad how it passes by so quickly. In just two months, I will enter my 40s. It makes me feel uneasy to be leaving my 30s behind. But I am comforted by the thought that I can strive to mature spiritually and mentally as I gain more experience.

I haven't yet received the letter you sent [about Eugene, Dennis, and their report card]. But I'm happy to hear they were doing well in school. Let's help them develop their potential as the Three Musketeers and do our best. Please congratulate them on behalf of their father.

You said the weather is getting cold there... But it's the end of March, and you are still wearing your winter clothes? I pray that everyone stays healthy and does not catch a cold.

I've been wanting to go to the bathroom since earlier and have been holding it, so I'll say bye bye for now and write again later.

Yours, who melts in your love in Regina!

2. Educating the children

I have three sons: Eugene, born in 1971, who lives in the Boston area; Dennis, born in 1974, who lives in the Vancouver area; and Jason, born in 1980, who lives in New York. When they were young, we moved around often and they had to transfer schools many times, but they adapted well. They were good kids who did well in school and listened to their parents. When I look back now, there are many things I wish I could have done for them, and many things I regret and am sorry for, but I am grateful that they grew up well.

When my children were young, I strongly believed they should take music lessons and play organized sports. Unlike in Korea, participating in extracurricular activities is considered important in Canada, and much was invested with the idea that it could provide lifelong benefits for the children. Violin, piano, clarinet, swim, soccer, baseball, hockey, taekwondo, football, wrestling, and marching band are just a few examples of the activities my children participated in while growing up.

After dinner, I had them practice piano one by one while I supervised. My mother was a church accompanist who taught me how to play, and I was following in her footsteps, teaching my sons for an hour every day. We put a lot of effort into finding the best teachers, and when they were learning to play the violin, I enrolled them in Suzuki classes. I started my youngest in violin lessons when he was still in diapers, and he learned like a sponge without finding it difficult. At the annual music competition, other participants would drop out of classes my children were registered in to avoid competing against them.

When they played hockey, it was difficult to get ice time at the arena, so their games were often scheduled early in the morning. I recall having to leave the house at four in the morning, getting them in the car while they were barely awake. At times I questioned whether I was putting too much pressure on them by prioritizing sports over sleep or making them practice piano or violin instead of doing homework. After they were grown, however, my children expressed their gratitude for the effort I put in, and my youngest even pursued a minor in violin while in university, making all the hard work worthwhile.

Eugene and Dennis took piano lessons from Janice Denike, who was considered the best teacher at the time. Both boys were talented pianists, so the lessons were well worth the money. Dennis had a competitive nature and achieved numerous awards at various piano competitions, even competing at the provincial level. In addition to his musical talent, he also demonstrated outstanding abilities in sports and was awarded a five-star rating in football. He was even offered an athletic scholarship to Queens University. He was also good at wrestling, and I remember him running around wearing a garbage bag to lose weight for matches. He did well in everything he was told to do, whether it was baseball or hockey, and always brought us great joy and pride.

Among the siblings, Jason had the greatest aptitude for music. When he was still a baby, I would take him along with us to his older brothers' piano lessons and he would crawl around under the piano and touch the pedals, much to the annoyance of their teacher. I don't know whether it was due to this early exposure to music, but at the music conservatory, a violin teacher and orchestra conductor named Mr. Kassian recognized that he had perfect pitch and suggested we have him take an IQ test, and the results confirmed that he was a genius. Mr. Kassian took him under his wing, and by the age of 4, he was performing as a violin soloist with the orchestra. He won many awards at various competitions, but because he was too small to carry his trophies from the podium by himself his teacher would have to go up there and carry the trophy for him. After moving to Vancouver, he would go up against college students in music competitions as a middle schooler and still manage to win.

While I poured most of my passion into providing my children with a strong foundation in music and athletics, their university education was also of great concern for me. My oldest son, Eugene, attended Campbell Collegiate in Regina. He got good grades, played the piano and clarinet, and was on the wrestling team, so he was a dependable eldest son. But our neighborhood was in a rural area where students were not highly motivated to pursue higher education. Most of them would become farmers after high school and would often start working while still in school. Furthermore, there was a cultural belief that it was shameful to not be independent after the age of 16, so Eugene followed the same path as his friends and took a job while in high school as a busboy, taking orders from the waiters. Trying to fit a job into a schedule already filled with music, sports, and schoolwork, he couldn't help but not have enough time for everything. Only I, as his mother, know how heartbroken I felt. I would cry while waiting outside the restaurant for him to finish his shift. Even if he had an exam the next day, he would work until midnight the night before, and I would feel like I was burning up inside. He had decided to go to Vancouver and should be preparing but since he was working... Fortunately, he got good grades and was able to get into UBC without incident. Although I was nervous at the time, I was proud and grateful for Eugene's independence and determination to do well in everything, from work and school to music and sports.

The youngest, Jason, has always excelled academically, so much so that his teachers repeatedly recommended that he skip a grade and when he graduated from middle school, he was named the top overall student in his class. At the graduation ceremony, his award was given last, and it recognized his outstanding performance in both academics and extracurricular activities. I remember I attended the ceremony alone and was busy moving about trying to take pictures to capture the moment. Because Jason was a brilliant student and because I wanted him to receive the kind of education that I couldn't provide for his brothers when we were living in the countryside, I sent him to a private school. Brentwood College

School, located in Mill Bay, near Duncan on Vancouver Island, was said to be the best, so I sent him there. At first, he didn't want to go because he didn't want to leave his friends, but I thought he should at least take the test, so I took him there. He did so well at the interview he was admitted on the spot, even though there was a waiting list. I still remember the principal remarking on how well he'd done, saying he'd never seen such high test scores. Jason continued to do well after being admitted to the school, gained acceptance to Yale, and worked at Goldman Sachs, making us proud. But Jason told me later he had bad memories from his high school years. It was not easy for him to adjust because most of the students were white and upper class and had known each other since middle school. It hurt me deeply to hear this after all the time that had passed... Even now, I get teary-eyed when I think about it. Nonetheless, I am grateful and proud that Jason persevered until the end without saying anything so as not to worry his mother.

When our children were very young, we all slept together in the same room. I thought they should grow up being given lots of love, so I didn't follow the Canadian cultural practice of putting the kids to bed separately or adhering to strict bedtime routines. People may not understand, but I thought it was healthy parenting to let the children eat and sleep comfortably and to raise them feeling secure in their parents' arms. When Eugene was a baby and we would turn off the lights to go to sleep, he would want to play more and call out, "Turn on the light, turn on the light," and we would have trouble going to sleep. We even purchased a crib

Eugene's 100th day celebration, 1971.

and a playpen and tried to put him to bed in them, as advised by Canadian parenting methods. But Dennis once fell out of the crib during a crying fit. After this incident, my resolve weakened, and we allowed our children to continue sleeping in our room. Although the shock at the time was so great I thought my heart stopped, luckily there were no serious injuries due to the fall.

Until the children were old enough to start attending school, we had them speak only in Korean and read and write in hangul. Despite their later complaints about the difficulties of learning English in school, I believe this laid a strong foundation for them to maintain their Korean skills throughout their lives. I remember once when we were living in Winnipeg and Dennis was about three years old and still learning to speak, I recorded a telephone conversation between him and his grandmother. When she asked

At my parents' house in Donggyo-dong, Seoul, Korea, 1974.

him what his mother was doing, he replied in Korean that his mom was sewing up a hole in his dad's underwear. It still makes me laugh every time I hear it. Whenever I visited Korea, I made sure to bring back Korean language books to go through with the children. I put in a lot of effort to ensure they would remember Korean and hangul. Although they now speak English, they can still understand everything they hear in Korean.

Since I had to work when they were growing up, I had to leave my children at daycare or with a babysitter. When we were living in Toronto, the older one was a big brother and was more reserved in nature, so he didn't cry as much, but his younger brother cried a lot. I would have to go to work, but he would chase me to the elevator, crying, "Mom, when are you coming back?" over and over again while clinging to my leg and eventually I would have to remove him in order to leave for work and I would wonder why I had to do this, and I would burst into tears. Even now my heart aches when I think about how Dennis cried. I worked hard to

Niagara Falls, 1974.

Harrison Hot Springs.

With the family of my second son, Dennis, at home in Port Moody.

With my grandson Owen.

At home with my family.

Family vacation in Mexico.

With my youngest son, Jason.

In the Rocky Mountains.

Lake Louise.

Family vacation in Mexico, December 2018.

provide for my children, but I regretted not being able to be there for them during those moments. Later, when they were grown, I told them I was sorry about all those times I had to leave them while they were crying so that I could go to work. They said they didn't even remember and it was okay. It continues to pain me that as a working mother, I could not fully care for my children, but I am grateful that they have grown up well.

My oldest son, Eugene, got married at the age of 34, and the middle child, Dennis, got married at the age of 32. When Eugene got married, there was an effort made by the mothers. My daughter-in-law's mother, Song Mi-ja, was a friend of mine from church in Korea. After she immigrated to the U.S., we lost touch, but once we reconnected, we began thinking, let's become in-laws.

We had been able to meet again through her father-in-law, Dr. Jeong Dae-wee, a remarkable man who had served as president of Konkuk University and the first president of the Korean National Commission for UNESCO. Dr. Jeong became first acquainted with my husband when he came across an article that my husband had written as a young professor in Toronto and gave it a glowing review, even having it published in the newspaper. Later, after Dr. Jeong's wife passed away, he married Kim Yeong-sil, whose daughter-in-law was Song Mi-ja. Both Dr. Jeong and Ms. Kim were the children of parents involved in the Korean independence movement and had been friends since they were seven years old. My friend happened to see a copy of my husband's book Tao Te Ching in Dr. Jung's library and remarked that she knew the author. We got back in touch and visited each other often. It feels all the more special that these connections and relationships came together and led to our children getting married.

Eugene is on the quiet side, but my daughter-in-law likes him. She has a bright personality and did well in school, having graduated from Amherst College and Columbia University Graduate School. She is also brave: through my friend Song Mi-ja, I had her send an email to my son Eugene. At first, they were a bit hesitant, but after two years of visiting each other every week in New York, where Eugene lived, and Boston, where my daughter-in-law lived, they wanted to get married.

My middle son, Dennis, saw his older brother marry a Korean person and perhaps wanted to do the same. At Christmas, while spending time with my daughter-in-law's friends, he made a connection with a friend, and the following year, we got another Korean daughter-in-law. They both now have two sons and are living happily, which brings me great joy.

A letter from my husband to our children

October 1, 1980

Dear Eugene and Dennis, my dear sons.

Thank you very very much for your wonderful letters, which were full of love, love, ♥ and ♥.

Yes, I miss you guys, too. I will be there in exactly 10 days. Maybe I might be there earlier than this letter. I am glad to hear that you like your new school. They are kind to you because you are good boys. Be kind to them too.

It is good for you to take piano lessons. Don't give up your violin, though. You can do both. Ask Mom to give you practice on both. You are doing good job, Eugene and Dennis. I am proud of you both, and Jason. I am the Father of three excellent young men, you guys!

Dennis, I have put your sunflower seeds on the shelf in my office, and whenever I see them, I think of you. I have also put your letter on the wall. I showed it to others, too. They all laughed especially because of your cute picture of you and me. They admired your neat handwriting too.

Eugene, you are a really great boy, baby-sitting Jason, and playing with Dennis. Say hello to your teachers for me. I will your letter on the wall, too.

Jason, nice baby! Grow fast and healthy. I will see you soon. (Read this to Jason! Eugene or Dennis.)

All you boys. Be good to each other and help Mom in all the possible ways!

Good-bye, See you soon!

With Love and Big Hug

Dad

6:00 p.m.

Oct. 1. 1980

My family has sent me heartfelt essays to celebrate the publication of my memoirs, and I include them here as a way of remembering who I am from their perspective.

Joanna (first daughter-in-law)

Dear Umunim,

For me, you've set a precedent within the family with your career and love for health.

At a time when some women didn't have the courage, the education, role models, or cultural backing to set out on their own and take charge of their career, you did. There are times in my own career when I feel I'm out of my element or I'm going down a path that is isolated, and then I think on the precedent and example that you have set. And you did it as an entrepreneur -- whereas my situation is within a company where I don't bear any of the direct financial risks. And you did it in Canada, that was at the time when you started out, very new to you in language, culture, and small business practices. More than the tremendous financial success you achieved through your business, what you've achieved in personal identity, exploration into life and people, and coming into your fuller being are what stand out to me as what your business success actually represents.

Your love of health is another aspect of who you are that stands out. There are some things that I can't exactly buy into -- like the oil pulling you've mentioned a few times :) -- but you do really believe that health is everything and you practice it. Not many people can practice health, but you really live it both through physical activities and also spiritual/mental/emotional practices. Not everyone has hobbies or personal interests that they invest time in. Or maybe they have hobbies/personal interests but they don't have the wherewithal to set aside the time. Or maybe they haven't listened closely enough to who they are to know what their real interests are. But I feel that you have, and you are a full person for it -- and as a result others around you get a better glimpse into who you are and perceive you as living a real life, with eyes and heart open.

I hope that my perspective shared here can shed further light into your life and the intangibles that you represent to me.

Humbly,

Joanna

Eugene (eldest son)

When I was little, our family moved around a lot, at times as often as once per year, from city to city all across Canada, but when I was 11 my dad got tenure at the University of Regina and we moved into the house we would live in for the next six years. The house was a three-bedroom bungalow wedged sideways into a narrow lot. In the backyard was a crabapple tree that my brothers and I would climb, and planted next to the front door, which was actually on the side of the house, was a lilac bush that blossomed each spring and had overgrown its space.

When I think about growing up in that house, I don't remember many idyllic days. It seemed there was always a piano lesson or clarinet lesson to hustle off to, homework to be completed, a recital looming on the horizon. There was also music theory class, and wrestling practice, or an early-morning hockey game, or marching band, taekwondo, or tennis. Yet I seem to remember we were able to have dinner together as a family each evening. My mom would sometimes make chicken wings in ketchup and soy sauce. That was a favorite.

In those years, as well as driving us to all of our various lessons and music festivals and recitals, in addition to doing all of the day-to-day tasks that go into raising three sons, my mom worked full-time at a Pinder's Drugs. For whatever reason, a lot of Roughriders went to that Pinder's to have their prescriptions filled and whenever one came in my mom would ask for his autograph to bring home for us.

There was a small, close-knit community of Korean-Canadian families living in Regina in those days and on many weekends there would be a gathering at somebody or other's house. There were holiday parties in the winters, picnics in Wascana Park in the summers, and there was one time my mom dressed in a hanbok and sang the Korean national anthem at a taekwondo tournament. In short, our life in those days was busy, bursting at the seams with activity, and at the same time small and mundane. I have a distinct childhood memory of walking into the kitchen one day during that time and finding my mom sitting alone at the table, gazing out the window above the sink that faced out over the driveway, at the sky high above the neighbor's house. She may have been daydreaming, she may have been pondering, or maybe she was wondering when this chapter in her life could be over and when her real life would begin.

As the saying goes, the days are long but the years fly by. Shortly after those days on Castle Road, with my brother Dennis moving to Vancouver for his first year at UBC, which I was also attending at the time, my mom decided it was time to pick up and get out of Regina as well, and from there events progressed as if according to plan: the purchase of the townhouse on Falcon Drive in Coquitlam, the obtaining of her license to practice in BC, the opening of her first pharmacy. The pharmacy was located in a strip mall down the street from the townhouse. It was a mile away from a Shoppers Drug Mart in one direction and a Pharmasave in the other. In fact, if I'm remembering correctly, the previous occupant was a pharmacy that had failed.

It took some time to build the business to more than 100 prescriptions in a day, which I remember we celebrated as a milestone, and then soon 100 prescriptions were like nothing. Within a few years, the pharmacy was generating enough income to send my brother Jason to a fancy boarding school on the Island and then to four years at Yale, and then after the final tuition check there was the purchase of a Mercedes-Benz S-class to replace her 10-year-old Honda.

It was also around this period she was launching into the next chapter of her life: community work and philanthropy. And as when she left Regina it was with that sense of bursting forth. She was assisting efforts to feed starving orphans in North Korea. She was helping to establish the Vancouver Korean-Canadian Scholarship Foundation. She was raising funds to help tsunami victims. She was donating a million dollars to a care facility for elderly Koreans, traveling to Seoul to receive a presidential citation, and being awarded a Queen Elizabeth II Diamond Jubilee Medal.

It has been my privilege to have been able to witness my mom's growth from working mother to business owner to philanthropist. Being so far removed out here on the east coast, I have missed out on many of her accomplishments, but many I have become aware of because with English being her second language she would ask me to edit the speeches she would make at various events, whether it was to welcome attendees at a VKCSF awards ceremony, introduce a VIP at a function, or deliver a keynote address. At times it felt like every communication I was receiving from her was a request to edit yet another speech. So, I am aware there have been many accomplishments.

In a curious coincidence, this assignment to write this essay comes in the same week I've been going over documents from the lawyer who is drafting Joanna's and my will and estate planning. So, thoughts about legacy have been on my mind lately, not just in terms of money and property -- our boys are probably not inheriting much more than the house they grew up in and a 2008 Subaru -- but more so in the form of beliefs and values, memories and traditions, and lessons. I hope my sons learn it is important to pursue their ambitions but there is also value in being decent and kind.

I still haven't got the recipe, if there is one, for the chicken wings my mom used to make, but there are of course so many things I have learned from her, both by her instruction and from her example. "Don't waste your time," she tells me. "Every moment is precious." To her, each day is an opportunity to go for a hike, play a round of golf, learn how to play the flute, swim laps at the pool, do something, anything. I know that she feels like there is so much more to do with her life, projects she wants to pursue that have timelines extending out 20 years. One lifetime is not enough.

Yet I would not be surprised to find that even time will not be able to contain her, and her legacy will be one that lasts for generations. She left a place that was too small for her and continues to make her mark in the world and in so doing nothing is impossible.

P.S. A letter to Mom

Congratulations, Mom, on the publication of your memoirs!

I'm sorry I snapped at you during that snowstorm in 2011 when you were waving gimbap in my face as I was driving on the interstate after I'd already said I didn't want any gimbap. As is often the case, it wasn't really about the gimbap, but regardless I shouldn't have responded the way that I did. Sorry.

And I'm sorry about the argument that time on the phone in 2019. The next day you wrote me an email, which I still have. You wanted a ribbon added to the flower arrangement you'd asked Joanna and her mom to order from the florist they were working with for the funeral. I knew from watching Korean dramas on Netflix why you thought the ribbon was important, but the florist, despite being Korean, didn't offer that service, didn't know anybody in the Boston area who did, and said nobody else who'd ordered from her had requested a ribbon. I couldn't understand why you wouldn't just let it go, but I shouldn't have blown up like that. It probably wasn't just about the ribbon.

And I'm sorry I doubted you that time in San Francisco in 1999, when you took all of us -- we were with Hugh's family and there must have been more than 12 of us -- to Fisherman's Wharf for dinner on the Fourth of July. I thought there was no way we'd be able to get a table without a reservation, but you went into Bubba Gump, located right on the water, and got us seated right away, right next to the window so that we were able to watch the fireworks show over the bay.

Several years ago, I was reading a biography of Steve Jobs, and as the writer described some of the things that made him who he was, I felt a jolt of recognition, the thought occurring to me that the founder of Apple was a lot like my mom! For example, there's your refusal to take no for an answer and the way you distort reality according to your will. There's your ability to make people do stuff they think can't be done, and how you play by your own rules.

Which is not to say that you park in handicapped spots like Steve Jobs reportedly did, but when we were growing up, we benefited in so many ways and on so many occasions because of who you were, as a mother, as a business owner, and as a person. You were right to push us despite all of the arguments, and you were right to insist, and to persist. Congratulations once again on the publication of your memoirs, sorry for those times I hurt your feelings, and thank you for being my mom. What you said in your email is true: I know how much you love me, and you are right to know I love you as well.

Your son, Eugene

Nathan (怡彦, older son of our eldest son, born November 25, 2007)

Among the memories I have with my grandmother is the somewhat regular occurrence of going to her apartment in the southwestern area of British Columbia, Canada, and to a room down the hall to the left of the entry of her condo, then to the first door on the right which is/was a storage room filled with stained wooden storage cases and tan brown cardboard boxes pushed up against the walls of the room. Within the room there were various things such as coins, pictures, watches, et cetera that one could look at for hours, which I did. As of now I'd be willing to bet that I've spent a good amount of time wandering around and looking at various pieces of the past with someone occasionally coming in and explaining the significance of a certain object, award, etc. that was related to her. I look back on those hours positively, and am glad to have had the opportunity to see a piece of my past and identity through my grandmother and that room.

Another pleasant memory of my grandmother was her thanking me for making her and her husband grandparents with my existence. Although this memory was horribly awkward at the time at the core it is heartwarming as she gave attention/ commendation for an event that no one intended and that I had nearly no part in. I feel it was quite thoughtful of her to take time out of the single week in which her three sons were with her to spend time even if brief, some positive attention.

Thomas (志彦, younger son of our eldest son, born January 15, 2011)

I've always felt like Halmuni has always been trying to keep us happy. One time when she was over in our town she took me and my brother to Toys R Us. She said we could pick anything we wanted and she would get it for us. To me, it was quite a special moment.

One of our traditions seems to be to go to a dim sum restaurant every time we visit Vancouver. Moments like these can make memories.

No matter what it seems all she wants for us is to let us have a good time, and I'm grateful for that, and I'm grateful for her.

Bonnie (second daughter-in-law)

Umunim,

Whenever someone talks about their mother-in-law, or rather, complains about them, I can never relate. After getting married, I moved in with you, father-in-law, and your parents. This would not be easy for any newly married woman, especially in a Korean household where my duties would automatically include cooking and cleaning for everyone. But after we got back from our honeymoon, you hired a cleaning lady so I wouldn't have to be burdened with the extra responsibilities. Being a newlywed came with its own challenges, so I was grateful that you didn't make my life harder, but tried to make it easier. Not all mother-in-laws are like that so I know I am very lucky.

You have many accomplishments, but I feel your greatest legacy is your sons and the men they've become. My biggest thank you is for Dennis. You have raised a man with a good heart that cares deeply for his family and friends. He's always trying to be a better husband, better father, and better friend. He is loving and I feel he knows how to love because he was so loved.

Before writing this letter, I made a list of the qualities I appreciated about you as my mother-in-law. That list consisted of: accepting, not controlling, not judgmental, understanding, doesn't hold onto negativity or resentment, and encourages happiness. Then I started thinking about my appreciation for you raising Dennis. I made a list of what I loved about him and I had an epiphany. The list is exactly the same! I see that his best qualities came from you. I am so grateful for this. I can only hope I can have such a positive and valuable impact on my children too.

Something else I'd like to emulate is that even with your busy schedule, you make sure to include something that you enjoy every day, whether it's golf or working on a passion project. Whenever you get back from a trip, the kids always ask,

"What did you do there?" and each time you answer, "I had a good time". It's an unexpected response to that question which makes us all chuckle every time but really, it sums it up perfectly. You had a good time. And honestly, I think the phrase sums up your life perfectly too. Your enthusiasm for life is delightful to witness and I hope Owen and James live their lives with the same intent.

I may not say it enough, but thank you for being a good mother to Dennis, a good grandmother to my children and good mother-in-law to me.

Bonnie

Dennis (second son)

Dear Mom,

I wanted to thank you for everything you do, but especially for teaching me the life lessons to live by: 1. prioritize health, 2. strive to keep learning, and 3. help others.

Firstly, you always prioritized health. Despite your incredibly busy schedule raising 3 sons, working as a full-time pharmacist while navigating a new language and culture in Canada, you still prioritized our health. You regularly made home-made lunches and dinners, and you kept us active with family swimming, tennis, and social events, as well as many of our other individual sports. When I got sick and hospitalized, you dropped everything and stayed by my side until I recovered. You made me feel safe and protected, confident that you would be there whenever needed.

Secondly, you made us learn and be fiercely curious. You helped us with all our school work, but also pushed us to learn music, sports, work ethic, how to treat others, lessons around money and business, and anything else we could. Arriving in Canada you learned English by watching soap operas on TV, and forty years later you suggested I learn Korean by watching Korean dramas on Netflix, which helps!

Thirdly, and perhaps most importantly, you taught me life was about helping others. You told me happiness can only be achieved by helping others. I see now the first and second lessons are important criteria to enable this ultimate goal. You can't help others if you don't learn, and you can't learn about anything if you're not well. But you can't be truly happy if you don't help others. I see now why you pushed so hard for me to become a doctor, as it keeps me engaged in all three of these principals. I've come to understand it is in helping others that one finds meaning in life. You always tell me to be happy, but I think what you are really telling me is to find meaning. Happiness is fleeting; it is the meaning that most of us seek.

Indeed, you have lived your life exemplifying these principles. You maintain exceptional health with great effort, swimming and walking every day. You even walked the El Camino de Santiago in Spain! You eat well, and your formal education is centerd around health. But you have also had a lifetime of learning, not only as a pharmacist but also in business, politics, and community development. You still strive to improve your golf swing! And most impressively to me, you have used your good health and education not as a means to improve your own life or status, but to help others. And what you have accomplished in helping your family, community, culture, and country is something to behold. I see all the meaning you have in your life, and you have not only provided me a proven path to achieve my own, but inspire me to achieve it. I am proud to say you are my mother.

Thanks mom, I love you.

Dennis

Owen (時彦, older son of our second son, born June 28, 2009)

Grandma,

Something I always look forward to is our family vacation to Mexico that you organize every year. I love being able to meet up with my cousins, aunts, uncles and you and grandfather in such a wonderful setting. For one week, we get to eat together, do fun activities, and enjoy each other's company. It's unfortunate that we all live so far apart but you are so thoughtful by making the effort to connect our entire family each year.

I love hockey, so going to an NHL game is extremely exciting for me. Whenever the opportunity arises for you to get NHL tickets, you immediately think of me and it makes me feel so special. I am lucky to have gone to many games now because of you. The most memorable game I've been to was when just you and I went together. We sat in the box where there was lots of free food and drinks. I was very impressed at how many burgers you ate. That game ended very late and it was a long drive from downtown but you still had a smile on your face until you dropped me off. Thank you for sacrificing your time (and sleep) solely to make your grandson happy.

It is one of the many incredible experiences you have given me. Whenever I see you, you are so encouraging and generous. You always tell me that I am so smart and I can achieve anything. It feels good to have someone believe in me like that. I'm very appreciative of all you do for me and I recognize that it's your hard work that has given me my comfortable modern life now.

Your grandson,

Owen

James (利彦, younger son of our second son, born October 11, 2011)

Dear Grandma.

I know family is very important to you. Our family lives across the world in different cities, so you always try to make plans to meet up in Mexico every year. I love going to Paradise Village to play with my cousins at the beach, play board games with my uncle, and eat good food. I'm grateful we have these vacations.

You are always proud of me. I know you're proud because you

always tell me great things when I get a good report card or score a goal in a hockey game. But even if I don't score a goal, you're still proud of me for trying.

I appreciate that you always want to buy me things. When I want something, you are so willing to buy it for me and try to make me happy.

I know you are very busy because you work, play golf, and do a lot of volunteer work, but when you make time to come to my events, you always make me feel special and loved.

Thank you, Grandma, for loving me.

Love,

James

Jason (youngest son)

Dear Mom,

Thank you for providing the opportunities I had growing up, and I'm sorry I didn't appreciate them enough at the time. I was too young to understand the early hardships in your career, and as I got older I took your later achievements for granted. Now as an adult with my own career, I can appreciate the challenges you had to overcome as an entrepreneur and small business owner, let alone as a woman and minority speaking a second language. I admire your perseverance and hard-won success in a time even less welcoming to diversity.

I've also realized just how much you had to learn for yourself along the way. Everything you taught me about Western culture and society - norms I've internalized having grown up immersed in them - you had to learn and adopt as an adult. I still remember your lesson on dinner etiquette during an Alaskan cruise with your parents, and it occurs to me I don't know where you would have learned that. I'm grateful for your curiosity and resourcefulness, and for your efforts to develop those qualities in me.

Congratulations on your biography. I'm glad people can read about your life and the impact you've had on so many others. You've always emphasized the importance of helping people, and I've seen how hard you've worked to live that mission.

Your loving son,

Jason

Chapter 5 :

Childhood

1. Korean War evacuation

When I was born, my parents lived in a large household with many relatives. My grandfather, Kang Heung-bin, and my grandmother, Jo Maria, along with their four sons and their families all lived together in what must have been a very large house located in a neighborhood at the foot of Namsan, and it was in this house that I was born. According to family lore, at the time of my birth, the family was gathered around the breakfast table, and I've been told that they expressed their congratulations and well wishes while having their meal.

Shortly after my birth, my father, Kang Si-ho, and my mother, Lee Ki-soo, and I moved to Donam-dong. According to my mother, when I was two or three years old, many of the neighbors complimented my appearance, saying that I was pretty, but I was so pretty, my mother was worried that someone would steal me and expressly forbade me from accepting candy from strangers. So, whenever I was told I was pretty and given a snack, I would scatter the treats in front of our house before going in, in compliance with my mother's instructions.

I was four years old when the events of 6/25 took place. At the start of the war, we continued to live in Donam-dong, and my father's youngest brother, who was a bachelor, sought refuge in the attic of our house from North Korean soldiers. Our neighbors were kind people, so even though they were aware of his presence, they kept silent, and I am very grateful to them. Then, on September 28, his oldest brother, hearing that peace had been restored, invited him to have naengmyun at Dongdaemun Market to celebrate. My youngest uncle was captured there, and to this day, no one knows what happened to him. According to another uncle who was a military officer, he was most likely shot in Miari Pass. In old photographs, my youngest uncle is the tallest and most handsome of the four brothers, and my older family members say he was particularly articulate and clear-minded and it was a shame to lose him. Additionally, he had been engaged for six months at the time, and there was his beautiful fiancee at home waiting for his return. I remember seeing my grandmother in her grief berating my oldest uncle for having called him to come out for no reason and getting him kidnapped. It remains a deep sadness buried within our family.

During the January-Fourth Retreat, my family also evacuated, and because one of my uncles was a military officer, we were able to travel by train. The conditions, however, were terrible. Women were unable to straighten their legs in the cramped space while the men rode on the roof, clinging to anything they could to keep from falling off. Every morning, they would check if everyone was accounted for and still alive. Fleeing for our lives, we eventually reached Busan. As all the refugees disembarked from the train, my grandmother on my mother's side stamped her feet and refused to get off. Because this was during an evacuation, the train was soon empty and there on the floor of the train was a bundle of newspaper, which she picked up and held to her chest as if it were the most precious thing. So that people wouldn't steal it, she had wrapped all her money in the newspaper to make it look like trash but then somehow misplaced the bundle somewhere on the train. Fortunately, the bundle was not taken by anyone and had remained undisturbed on the floor, so it appears my grandmother's trick worked.

In Busan, we boarded an LSD for Jeju Island with the help of Ryu Je-han (English name: George Henry Rue), an American missionary physician who was the director of the Samyuk Seoul Hospital, which would later become Sahmyook Medical Center, and whose patients included President Syngman Rhee. I later learned that at that time North Korean forces had advanced to the Nakdong River and it was feared that all of South Korea was about to fall, so refugees were being taken farther south to Jeju Island. Then General MacArthur successfully landed at Incheon and helped save the country. Anyway, many South Korean refugees were evacuated to Jeju Island, where each family was assigned to take care of one refugee family. During that time, the people of Jeju Island took good care of the refugees as if they were family, for which we will be eternally grateful, and later, when I had become a university student, I went back to visit with my mother.

The people who were assigned to take care of my family were kind, and I remember being treated very well. At that time, my mother was just over 30 years of age, and had been a teacher at Deokseong Girls' High School. After I was born, she quit and started running the household. So the kitchen was relatively unfamiliar to her. One morning, after our arrival on Jeju Island, she'd gone into the kitchen to make rice for breakfast and found a large snake. She screamed, and everyone in the household came running. On Jeju Island, however, these large snakes were considered divine beings that served as guardians of the houses, so there was one in every home. The members of the household found it amusing that this newcomer from Seoul was so frightened and they returned to their rooms as if nothing had happened.

Also in the kitchen, there was a large urn filled with water, and seeing that there was a lot of sediment that had accumulated at the bottom, my mother decided she would wash the urn and fill it with fresh water. My mother was happy to do it, thinking she was doing a good deed for the family taking care of them, but the grandmother flew into a rage, because on Jeju Island, it was believed that if the accumulation at the bottom of the urn was removed, the family would be ruined. My mother did not know this. These are some of the memories of my mother from when she was a spirited young woman on Jeju Island, where she used to steal away to her room to wipe away tears in secret. Nonetheless, I admire her foresight in packing a sewing machine amidst the chaos of evacuating. With the machine, she was able to sew hanbok jackets for the local residents and use them to barter with for seafood caught by haenyeo from the bottom of the sea.

We left Jeju Island after about a year and returned to the mainland. I have many fond memories from the time we spent there. I love the ocean so much that I once remarked to my husband that I must have been a fish in a previous life, and he replied that maybe it was because I'd had a good experience on Jeju Island when I was young.

Back on the mainland, we settled first near Busan in Deoksan, where I attended first grade, and from there we moved to Jinhae, which is where the Korean Naval Academy is located. My father operated a miniature golf course near the academy, and the place would get very crowded with navy cadets on weekends. The course had 18 holes just for putting, but it was well maintained and had a fountain with goldfish. I remember playing golf with the navy cadets and winning chocolate as a prize. Jinhae is quite far from Seoul, so whenever we went to visit my grandmother or grandfather, we would have to board the train at dawn and arrive late at night.

During our time in Jinhae, when I was in second grade, I experienced a difficult period when my legs became paralyzed. As a young child, I had a poor appetite, and my mother would have a hard time getting me to eat. After school, she would take me to have jjajangmyeon and she would give me all kinds of herbal medicines. If a seller claimed a medicine was effective, she would buy it and give it to me. One time, she was told raw ginseng would increase my appetite, so she gave it to me. Later, as we were returning from church one day, my legs suddenly stopped moving and I couldn't cross a ditch. My mother was frantic and put me on her back and ran from hospital to hospital. While I slept, she stayed by my side crying and praying, and it was all a big commotion. Eventually, a doctor successfully treated my condition with a vitamin B injection. During rehabilitation, my mother and father wanted me to do well, and motivated me by saying, "If you can reach this far, I'll give you money," and they would pass me bills one by one. Even then, I liked money, so I worked hard. I can still see the two of them clapping their hands in joy during my stretching exercises as they saw me get better and better. By the end, I had collected a stack of the money my parents gave me, and I think I was able to be successful in my rehabilitation due to their support. Also, because of all the herbal medicines my parents gave me when I was young, I am now known for having a healthy appetite.

2. Childhood

I attended Dochun Elementary School in Jinhae until the end of third grade, and then we moved to Seoul and I started fourth grade at Jaedong Elementary School. When I was going to school in Jinhae, my classmates would tease me because of my Seoul accent, but in Seoul, I became a Gyeongsangnam-do negi. I remember that when I had to go to the front of the class to introduce myself as a new student, my classmates giggled because I spoke in a Gyeonsang-do dialect. They even urged me to sing for them, thinking it would be funny, so I sang a frog song with all my heart and stuck my tongue out at the end. They thought that was hilarious, and we had a lot of fun.

Since it was a new school, I initially didn't know where the restroom was, and when I couldn't locate it, I ended up running back home. But I quickly adjusted and made friends and spent time with them at my house. I used to enjoy cleaning time at school when my friends and I would use candle wax to polish the floors. One of my friends was a jokester, and once while walking in front of a group of boys she strutted forward, exclaiming, "Ladies first," before slipping and falling, much to her embarrassment. Since our classes were not co-ed in fourth grade, we knew little about boys, and I thought it was brave of her to attempt something like that.

When my family first moved to Seoul, my mother stayed back

in Jinhae to take care of some things related to the miniature golf course business. Meanwhile, my father and I stayed at my grandmother's house. Perhaps because I was still young, I had trouble falling asleep by myself, so I slept in my grandmother's room. Even though she could be a tiger grandma at times, she was always loving and kind to me.

My father would come home from work and help me with my studies. We would stay up late into the evening going over my homework, and he would explain the material that I was having trouble with. I think he was worried that I might fall behind because I came from the countryside, so he took it upon himself to make sure that didn't happen. Even when he must have been exhausted from work, he remained dedicated to my education. If I started to doze off, he would tell me to go out and wash my face, and although he could be stern, he would often come home with chocolates, toys, and other kinds of gifts to comfort and support me. Thanks to my father's warm love, I was able to thrive in my new school.

After my mother moved to Seoul, my father was always busy with work but he always made time for my mother and me on Sundays. I have fond memories of trips to Onyang Hot Springs in the winter and hiking up Dobangsan with beer and watermelon in the summer. We would splash around in the water and have a great time. And when we returned to the city, my father would take us out for hamheung naengmyeon. That naengmyeon was so delicious that even now I try to go back often to have it. For me, hamheung naengmyeon tastes like the happy times I spent eating with my parents.

After my mother joined us in Seoul, we lived in a house in Anguk-dong. All the other houses in the neighborhood were hanoks, but ours was a two-story house, so I could look out the window of my room on the second floor and see far into the distance. I loved that view, so I always kept my window open. When I go back now, the hanoks are all gone and the house has been converted into a traditional tea house. Although there have been a lot of changes over the years, I'm happy that visitors to the teahouse can still enjoy the same magnificent view that I once did from my bedroom window.

The attic of the house was filled with food, and, when we had guests, I would crawl up into the attic even though no one asked me to and bring down all the food and serve it to the guests. And in the alley behind the kitchen there were shoeshine boys, and I remember I would give them the pastries my father bought rather than eating them myself. My mother was embarrassed, but when I think about it now, I think I learned from her, who was always volunteering with the church and feeding others, and my father was the type of person who if he saw somebody was cold on the street he would take off his coat and give it to them.

When I was young, I did not have much of an appetite for some reason, and my mother would always pester me to eat. If I was leaving for school without having breakfast, she would follow me with a bowl and a spoon, trying to get me to eat at least a little.

When she cooked, she worked hard to make delicious food that she thought would appeal to my taste buds. At that time, it was common for children to have head lice, but my mother went to great lengths to ensure I didn't get them. She tied my hair up nicely, dressed me in nice clothes, and spared no expense to shower me with all her care. I grew up nourished by my parents' love. I don't think I will ever forget the grace of their love.

In preparation for middle school, I attended a cram school and studied hard, and I remember the instructor being very nice to me. Seeing me busily running about with my hair tied up in a ponytail, she gave me the nickname "Squirrel" and thought I was cute, and during that difficult time of studying for the middle school entrance exam she took care to make sure I was doing all right. Of course, I regret not taking private tutoring lessons, which would have helped me do better. At that time, many students received extra help from private tutors, so my mother asked whether I would like to do likewise, but I remember declining, because I had once been hit by a tutor with his fist on my head. I don't know what happened, but a well-known tutor came to our school and was helping a group of students. Without thinking, I was just sitting there and looking on, when the tutor hit my head with his fist, which made me so angry... That is why I didn't want a private tutor, but it turned out to be an opportunity to study hard on my own.

When we lived in Anguk-dong, we used to gather with our relatives at my grandmother's house every week to make tofu. I have happy memories of the savory flavor of that tofu that I can't have now and the sound of the family filling the house. I think it was because I was surrounded by such loving family members that I was able to adjust quickly to my new school and grew up never feeling lonely despite being an only child.

My grandmother had a reputation in the neighborhood as a tiger mother-in-law, and all three of her sons lived near her in Anguk-dong, so whenever she said, "Come eat tofu," everyone in the family would hurry to her house. My grandmother's tofu was delicious, and she was skilled at making it, but, when I look back now, I realize my aunt put in a lot of effort to take care of everything. My grandmother on my mother's side was very old-fashioned and had curly hair and wore a white hanbok, but my grandmother on my father's side was a modern woman. Even in the 1950s she had short hair and wore a pink overcoat. When she was younger, she was widely admired for her beauty. I've been told my cousins were beautiful because they resembled her, but I feel that I only inherited a small fraction of her beauty.

Despite her reputation for being strict, my grandmother held a special fondness for me, perhaps because of my father, who supported the household. At the time, my father earned a good income, and when he gave her money, she would evenly distribute it among her three sons, who would kneel before her to receive their share. My father's support must have meant a great deal to her. Whenever there was a big family event, we would gather at my grandmother's house for a meal, and there would be a table for the sons and another for the women, and my grandmother would always have me at the sons' table. At other times, when I said I had no appetite except for naengmyeon, she would take me to Wooraeok even though it was snowing so I could have naengmyeon.

I've heard that my grandmother converted to Christianity early on in her life and it was a church elder who introduced her to my grandfather and brought them together. That is how my grandmother, from the Jo family in Seoul, came to marry my grandfather, who was the son of a landowner in Pyongpyong. My grandfather would read the Bible all day long, and I remember him saying it was so delicious he licked his lips while reading. He was a landowner in Pyonggang-gun, Gangwon-do, and he followed the Pyonggang custom of slaughtering cattle at midnight and then afterward sharing kkwong naengmyeon with everyone, including the servants. He was a man with a generous heart who regarded his household staff as family. His hometown is now in North Korea. When the North Korean army came, it ordered the landowners to move into the servants' quarters and the servants to take the landowner's room, but his household staff remained extremely protective of him.

According to family lore, my grandmother was so tough that during the division of North and South Korea and amidst all the turmoil of that time she went back and forth across the DMZ to bring goods from Pyonggang to the south. It was an incredibly dangerous task that could have led her to being caught at the military demarcation line, but she risked it to protect the family's assets. She was truly a brave woman who served as a strong foundation and center of our family, along with my grandfather. Thanks to them, we could all lead solid lives.

My childhood memories of growing up with my cousins as one big family fills my heart, and we continue to have close friendships and speak to each other like siblings. Even though my grandmother gave me favorable treatment back then, the others didn't seem to mind, and we got along well. Our good relationship continues to this day, and I am grateful for that. I remember giving my cousins various items without the grownups knowing. They would ask for things like toys, pocket money, or chocolate, and I, not fully grasping the concept of scarcity, would give it to them without hesitation. Perhaps that is why my cousins didn't resent me as much.

I have a memory of playing yut with my cousin Wan-sook, whose name used to be Hwa-ja before she changed it, at my older uncle's house while my parents were out running errands. Playing with my cousins was always enjoyable, but on that day, I kept winning and Wan-sook became angry and scratched my face. When my parents returned and saw the scratch, there was a big commotion, and Wan-sook was severely scolded. When we were young, we played together and got into trouble, and that's how we grew up. Now, my cousin has been struggling with chronic back pain, so I often call her on the phone, and we talk about our lives. Our shared memories of growing up together as children connect us like a string.

I was also close with my cousin Myung-ja, who was the daughter of my younger uncle. Our fathers had a good friendship, which I think also brought us closer. Because my parents had no son, Myung-ja's younger brother grew up in our home, a common arrangement in those days when sons were valued. I was close with my cousins, so the situation felt natural for everyone. He eventually went to medical school in Seoul and is now an orthopedic surgeon. I feel that this special connection to my younger uncle's family has further strengthened our bond.

My extended family on my mother's side was also close, and we often gathered. Whenever a family member had a birthday, we would all make the trip to my grandmother's house in Sinseol-dong to celebrate. Our frequent gatherings allowed us to have a great influence on each other. One of my uncles on my mother's side went to study in the United States with the encouragement and support of American missionaries from the Seventh-day Adventist church where my grandfather, Pastor Lee Sung, served as its first leader. Following in my uncle's footsteps, many of my cousins also went abroad to study, which naturally sparked my interest in doing the same.

During my elementary and middle school years, my cousins from my aunt's family would spend their vacations at our house, and we were practically like siblings. Looking back, I now realize that my mother invited them over to help my aunt, who was struggling to raise five children. My uncle was a graduate of

Dongkyung University in Tokyo, Japan, and a professor who taught at the Seoul National University College of Engineering, but he was often ill due to his poor health. Since I tended to eat a lot more when my cousins were around, my mother was happy to have them over. Thanks to my mother's kindness, I have wonderful memories of spending happy times with my cousins. Even outside of school vacations, we often saw each other, spending time together and playing, and as I've gotten older, I've come to appreciate how fortunate I was to have such a close-knit family while growing up.

I have a cousin, Choi Choong-up, on my mother's side who is the same age as me, but because I was born a few months earlier, the grownups told him to call me "older cousin," so he still calls me that to this day. When we were young and all of the cousins were gathered at my grandmother's house in Sinseol-dong, we would all sleep together in one room. During middle school, we didn't see each other as much, but we reconnected when we were university students and sang together in the church choir. When I first met my husband, the three of us would hang out together, and we became close again. We recently met again and spent a wonderful time reminiscing. It felt like old times all over again.

3. Middle and high school

I remember how much fun it was in middle and high school to be with my friends, and how it felt like the whole world. When I think back to those days, the first things that come to mind are the conversations I had with my friends, whether it was at school or church, and the memories of hanging out with them. Those friends are still with me today as lifelong companions, and even now I can tell what they are thinking just by looking at their faces. It is a wonderful blessing to have friends with whom you can pick up right where you left off, as if you just saw them yesterday, even after not seeing them for an extended period. My memories of studying and serving in the church with my friends are like sweet candies that I have collected and secretly take out to eat to give me strength when I am going through a difficult time.

When I attended Kyunggi Girls' Middle School, I had a classmate named Lee Jong-hwa, and we became best friends. She lived near my house in Anguk-dong, so we used to make the trip to and from school together. Her family was not well off and she had four younger siblings, so my mother took her in and practically raised her as her own. Consequently, my memories of that period are filled with spending time with my friend and studying together for exams. Since I devoted so much of my time to church activities, my friend had better grades than me, and when we studied together, I would often fall asleep while she stayed up all night.

When my mother would tell us to turn out the lights and go to sleep, we would duck under blankets so the light wouldn't escape and study like that. Sometimes when we got hungry, we would tear pieces of kimchi and eat them with rice in secret, and just thinking about how delicious that was makes my mouth water.

While walking to school in the morning, we would see students from other schools, such as Sookmyung and Joongdong, as well as Kyunggi. Down a particular alley, we would have to maneuver through a horde of boys heading in the opposite direction, but the two of us were undaunted and marched through the crowd with confidence. Our school instilled in us a sense of pride, so we would walk with even more confidence. My friend went on to study at Seoul National University College of Pharmacy, and when my uncle was president of Sahmyook University, she became a professor of pharmacy there and even served as a dean. When Jong-hwa talks about my family, she calls them Mom, Father, and Uncle, and we are truly like family and remain best friends even to this day.

When I was in my second year of middle school, the 4/19 uprising occurred, and on that day all of the students had to be picked up from school to go home. My father sent a car to pick me up, and the scenes I witnessed from the back of the jeep on the ride home remain etched in my memory. School bags were scattered all over the intersection at Gwanghwamun, and students who appeared not much older than me lay on the side of the road. It was truly an indescribable horror. I was in my third year of middle school at the time of the 5/16 military coup... Having witnessed the nation's painful history firsthand, I can truly appreciate the preciousness of our country's achievement of democracy.

I read a lot of novels during middle school. At the time, it cost 100 won per day to borrow a book, and I found them so enjoyable I would stay up all night reading. Even now, when I am engrossed in a good book, I lose track of time and read late into the night. One of my favorite authors during middle school was Pearl Sydenstricker Buck, and I read every one of her books. The Japanese novel Oshin was another favorite that stayed with me for a long time. Thinking back on the books I loved makes me reflect on my life up until now. Oshin depicts the life of a woman who grew up poor in Japan. The protagonist struggles to survive by eating barley rice when there is no food, and eventually succeeds in business despite the hardships. I thought it was impressive that a woman could still be engaged in business even past the age of 80. I sometimes wonder if the influence of that book is why I am still working so hard like this.

I also have happy memories of the trio I sang with at church. We were all born in 1946, the year of the dog, so we all went by nicknames that were dog-related: Jang Myung-hee was Bulldog, Choi Hee-sook was Badoogy, and I was Puppy. Hee-sook and I had the same birthday, so I felt like we had a special connection. The three of us were invited to perform as a trio at various events, and we were always happy to accept. As we practiced for our performances, our hearts and minds seemed to harmonize like we were matching our pitches. Whenever we were together, we

Seoul Joongang Church Choir, 1966.

Front row from left: Song Mi-ja (mother of first daughter-in-law), Badoogy (Choi Hee-sook), Puppy (Kang Yoo-soon), and Bulldog (Jang Myung-hee).
Back row from left: Choi Seung-kook, Jeon Soo-myung, Nam Dae-gak (later president of Sahmyook University), and Choi Seung-kwan.

were always happy and comfortable. There was a time when we made a mistake while performing, and I was embarrassed. At the time, my face turned red and I didn't know how we managed to finish, but when I look back now, it has become a cute and funny memory.

There was a group of six of us who were especially close in school, and I have one particular memory of us spending an entire night together. At the time, there was a curfew in place, so we always yearned for the chance to stay out past midnight. The curfew was lifted on December 24th and 31st, so that was our chance. We booked a room at a motel for December 24th and made a pact to stay up all night. We went to Namdaemun Market where foreign candies and snacks were sold and we bought marshmallows, the most popular item at the time, and strolled around Myeong-dong while eating the marshmallows. We even ventured to the top of Myeong-dong Cathedral and rubbed our sleepy eyes as we talked. At around three or four in the morning, however, we were unable to resist our sleepiness any longer, despite our goal to stay up all night, and eventually we all dozed off. Being with your friends is just so much fun, and I still feel happy today because of the memories I have.

I also have some amusing memories of playing pranks on our teachers. For example, we would rest a chalkboard eraser on top of the classroom door and wait for the teacher to come in, causing the eraser to fall on them. One time, before algebra class, we put our chairs on top of our desks and hid underneath, so when our teacher, who was a young bachelor fresh out of college, entered the room, he was puzzled to find what appeared to be an empty classroom and went to the office to inquire. When he returned, we were back in our seats, as if nothing had happened, leaving him further confused. We played so many pranks on our teachers, our grade came to be known as the Texas Division. We were born in 1946. Our parents thought the name was fitting because we arrived during that joyful period after Korea was liberated from Japan and could finally be free.

I also have memories of our gym teacher, Mr. Shin, who was very intimidating. He would whack us with the attendance book if we misbehaved. At that time, none of the other teachers used corporal punishment nor were there students who misbehaved that badly, so getting hit was a memorable experience. Our school had a swimming pool, and during class, we were required to swim from one end of the pool to the other. Halfway across, I would often feel exhausted and unable to go any further, but instead of helping, Mr. Shin believed in tough teaching. So, I have several memories of almost drowning. Now it's all memories, so when I talk to my old friends from those days, we often reminisce about our experiences with Mr. Shin. I don't know whether it's because of those experiences, but I now swim laps every day at dawn.

My English-language teacher was Kim In-gyeong, and I remember impressing her by reciting several pages of text we had learned in class and doing well on the test. And during a part of the class when we would sing songs in English, I sang Que Sera,

Sera, and my teacher was worried about whether that was an appropriate song for children to sing. Looking back now, I think I was a cheerful student.

4. Missionary work during college

Church has always been at the center of my memories from the time I was very young. Accompanying my parents to church was a weekly routine, and even when we had to flee to Jeju Island and Jinhae, we never missed a Saturday service. It was through these experiences that I learned the values of the church and grew up naturally immersed in them. When I was in middle school, most of my friends from church went away to Sahmyook Middle School, leaving me to attend church alone, but the college students in the church took me under their wing and brought me along to their church activities. We sang in the choir together, taught Sabbath school, and ate together after service. It was through these

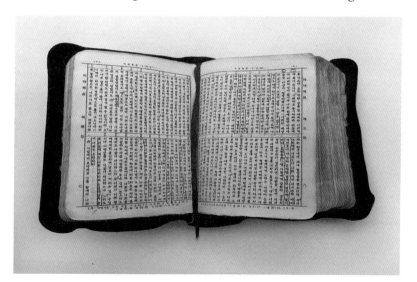

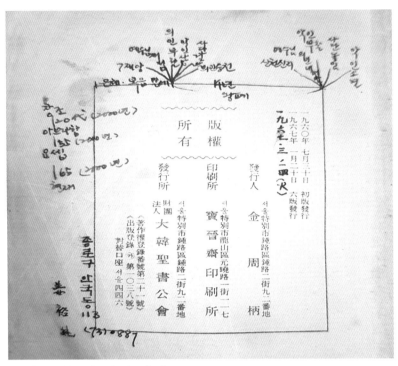

The Bible I still have from back in the day.

experiences that I felt a sense of belonging and connection with the church community that has lasted to this day.

At the time, Song Gil-jang and Choi Jun-myung, both Seoul National University students, were the youth leaders at Cheonjin-dong Church. Despite my young age, they entrusted me with the same responsibilities that they would give to other college students. Kim Kyung-ja and Sun-woo Jin-ju were also always looking out for me. Looking back, I realize that it must have been quite burdensome for them to take care of a young child like me, but they never showed it and became my friends, which is a testament to their pure hearts. We would often have sincere discussions about God, and I believe their influence had a significant influence on my parents' faith becoming my own. Despite our age difference, we remained friends and talked about our faith and our studies and comforted each other during difficult times of service activities. That's why they're still precious friends to this day. We recently met in Los Angeles, and thanks to our shared fellowship and religious life, we were able to open our hearts and speak comfortably to each other, just like back then.

When I was in my first year of middle school, I taught a group of elementary school students in Sabbath school, and one of those students later came to Vancouver and contacted me, saying I'd been their teacher when they were in sixth grade. Other students from around that time have gone on to become pastors and mentioned in their sermons that I'd been their Sabbath school teacher, and others visited me as professors. It is heartwarming to see how much they've grown, even though we were only a few years apart in age, and to know that I remain a good teacher in their memories. Looking back, I realize that in order to teach them I had to study the Bible diligently and be active in church life and I grew from having that experience. And to receive their gratitude from these friends, there can be no greater gift than that.

As someone who never missed a worship service, I feel that the church is my home and my home is the church. The seat at the piano is a particularly familiar place for me among the various areas of the church. I have played as an accompanist for different worship services at the church, though there was a piano major who played for the main worship service. Inspired by my mother's devoted work for the church, I started playing the piano at church and eventually came to view it as a valuable mission. I felt that playing the piano was my number one task because singing hymns without accompaniment was unacceptable. When the congregation's voices blended with the piano's sound to fill the church, I would imagine how pleased God must be and play with greater diligence. I also enjoyed listening to the pastor's sermons from my seat at the piano. I have fond memories of listening to the sermons, hearing the gentle voices of the congregants responding with "amen," and watching my mother joyfully dedicating herself to the church's work and living by God's word.

When I was a college student, there was a significant surge in the number of college-aged congregants at the Seventh-day Adventist Church, thanks to the evangelism efforts of Pastor Moon Sun-il. Attending the evangelism meetings was a truly fulfilling experience for me as I worked to strengthen my faith and deepen my relationship with God. As the church's membership grew, more college student clubs formed, and I continued to be active, serving as the accompanist, singing in the choir, participating in evangelism activities, and volunteering. I was also an enthusiastic member of the MV youth group, where I sang with fellow members at worship, taught Sabbath school, helped make ddukguk and serve lunch after service, went door-to-door to evangelize, and practiced my faith with such fervor that it would be difficult to replicate.

I served as vice president of a student association of Seventh-day Adventists in the Seoul area and sang with the Seoul Union Immanuel Choir. The choir was occasionally invited to sing at evangelism meetings, and we would gather at the headquarters in Hoegi-dong to practice. In such ways, I continued my religious life with my fellow college students. Once, while I was evangelizing at an intersection in Jongno, a professor from Ewha Womans University who happened to be passing by, spotted my university badge and asked if I could perhaps remove it. When I was younger, I was just a child holding onto the hem of her mother's skirt as she went to church, but during college, my faith matured to the point where I stopped studying on Saturdays and dedicated myself to the church.

One of my most memorable experiences is our mission trip to Ganghwa Island. I was part of a team of about 20 youth members who traveled there to spread the gospel. We felt a strong desire to share God's love with the locals, so we went door to door, cleaning outhouses, assisting farmers, and gathering the children around for study lessons and feeding them snacks. We did our best to serve the community through our volunteer work. The evangelism meetings we held every evening were well attended by the local residents. We taught them about the Bible and worshipped together, spreading God's love. Even now, the sound of insects in the fields in summer transports me back to Ganghwa Island, where we worked our hardest without being aware of the heat. When I must speak at large events these days, I think I am able to do it without being nervous because of my experience preaching the word in front of so many people during that time.

At Ewha Womans University, there were chapels for the whole school, and each college had its own chapel. At the pharmacy school's chapel, I went up to the podium and talked about the Bible, and the students enjoyed listening to the Bible stories. At that time, the church was the top priority in my life, and with the church being such a focus, I grew to know and love the Bible, which allowed me to tell stories from it naturally as a matter of course. I even started an SDA student association in which we read and shared Bible verses at lunchtime. During these meetings, the Word was truly alive as we shared it with each other and found ways to implement it in our daily lives. We prayed for and supported each other. I read the Bible so much that the pages of the small Bible I carried around with me became tattered. I read it in its entirety once or twice a year, so it was only a slight exaggeration to say I always had a Bible in my hands. I even completed the highest level of Bible study at church. When I was younger, my grandfather used to tell me how much he enjoyed reading the Bible, and I now understood deeply what he meant.

My mother's influence was the biggest reason why I attended church with such fervor. When I was a child, she would often have to lie down in her bedroom at home due to her weak health. At church, however, she cooked noodles for the congregation,

made multiple batches of kimchi, donated 500 million won for church construction, and fed hungry children and provided for their education. She lived according to the teachings she learned at church. Watching her from up close, I could only follow her example and learn from her life. When I was in college, however, my mother was often in the hospital for back surgery. She underwent four procedures at Severance Hospital, and during those times, she practically lived there. As part of our daily routine, my father and I would stop by to see her in the morning, and then after school, I would go with my father to see her before we returned home.

When I was a sophomore in college, my mother came close to

dying during surgery. I recall how my hands were shaking so badly that even simple tasks like opening or locking the door felt difficult. In that precarious moment, the entire church prayed for my mother, and young members of the church visited the hospital to pray for her recovery. One young person, in particular, would come every day at dawn to pray. Our collective prayers reached the heavens, and to everyone's relief, my mother made it through the crisis. I cannot express how overwhelmed I felt. I have witnessed the power of intercession, so whenever I hear a fellow church member is going through a difficult time, I immediately offer my prayers and support.

During a period when I was discovering the joys of prayer, I would wake up at four in the morning to attend morning prayer meetings. As I walked from Anguk-dong to Changjin-dong at dawn, I sang hymns, and I would be so excited for the conversation I was going to have with God that day that even walking in the dark did not frighten me. I think I was happier then because I had a pure heart. At that time, I climbed to the top of the hill at Samcheong Park every morning with my younger brother, exercised there, drank water from the spring, and ate the soft tofu that was sold there. The memories of our conversations while climbing the hill are very precious to me. Even now, I wake up at dawn every day, and I cherish this time of day when my mind and soul are clear, thanks to my childhood memories.

Without a doubt, the church and the Bible form the cornerstone of my existence. Although I initially attended church because of my parents, my encounters within the church have molded my worldview, mentality, approach towards life, and principles, all of which still anchor me today. Through my journey in understanding God's love, I have cultivated trust and affection for others, and found a clear purpose and path for my life.

5. Visit to Israel

The experience of attending the World University Festival in Israel as a representative of Korean university students during my fourth year of university was a significant turning point for me. I had not been interested in studying abroad, but this experience made me realize its importance. Meeting university students from all over the world was a special experience that broadened my narrow worldview, which had been limited to domestic experiences -- I was the proverbial frog in the well. Through the church, I'd had the opportunity to meet foreign missionaries, and the fact that all of my close cousins had left to study abroad, influenced by my uncle who was a professor at Sahmyook University, also had an impact on me. Until my visit to Israel, however, foreign countries were a world that I had not directly experienced. Now it became a vividly real world that deeply touched my life.

In the spring of my senior year at Ewha, we heard an international student conference was being held in Israel, and one of my professors wanted to nominate me as a student representative. It was not an easy decision, however, as the cost to attend would exceed $3,000. My mother was concerned about the expense, but my father did not hesitate to support me, and I joined the Korean delegation. There were four of us. From Ewha, there were Jang Sun-young, a student in the College of Art who was the daughter of the director of the Seoul City Mental Hospital in Cheongnyangni, Kim Myung-shin, an English major whose father was Kim Sang-yup, the president of Korea University, and me, and the fourth student in the group was Hong Song-il, a Seoul National University student majoring in foreign affairs.

In Israel.

With Jang Sun-young, Kim Myung-shin, and dean of students Kim Jeong-han (center), 1968.

Ewha's president, Kim Ok-gil, had reservations about letting us travel alone, so we were accompanied by Kim Jeong-han, the dean of students. Ms. Kim was a strict disciplinarian and an intimidating presence, but we also saw her warm and caring side during our time abroad as she looked after us. Before our departure, she expressed concern over my appearance, thinking that I looked skinny and frail. But during the entire visit, I was in the best of health, and she was surprised by my endurance. In preparation for the trip, my father took me to Songok Dress Shop in Myeong-dong and put together outfits for me to wear in Israel. The shop owner was so impressed with my father's selections that he thought he was an artist. The other students in our delegation didn't bring many clothes, assuming they would be shopping for them overseas, but the selection wasn't as great as they had anticipated, so they wore just the same clothes. In contrast, my father had prepared me with a whole wardrobe of tailored outfits, so when I look at pictures from that time, I believe I look like the most fashionable one of the group (although that is just my opinion). It is a cherished memory of my father's love for me.

Upon our arrival in Israel, I was amazed by the sheer number of university students from all around the globe, enough people to fill two coach buses. And it was my first time seeing an orange. In Korea, I'd eaten tangerines but never an orange. During breakfast, the European students sitting next to me showed me how to peel an orange, and for some reason the memory of that morning has stuck with me. The highlight of the itinerary was the pilgrimages to the holy sites. We visited Bethlehem, the birthplace of Jesus Christ, and Mount Sinai, among other holy sites in Egypt. When we reached the site of Jesus' crucifixion, I was moved to tears. As someone who was so immersed in the church, being able to visit these holy sites was a special and unforgettable experience that left my heart trembling. Even now, I can distinctly remember walking in the footsteps of Jesus, seeing the scenery, and the emotions that overwhelmed me.

During our time in Israel, there was a great opportunity for cultural exchange. Each delegation had a chance to showcase their country's cultural traditions in a large concert hall. Prior to our arrival, we had taken lessons to prepare for the performance, including singing lessons from Lee Ki-jong, who was the choir director at my church, and folk-dance lessons. Although I wasn't very skilled, I did my best to prepare. Ms. Kim was so nervous watching us on stage she could hardly stand it, but I was thrilled to be up there as a representative of Korea, introducing our country to the world. We performed Arirang in our hanboks. Seeing the eyes of the international audience on us, I felt my confidence grow, and for the first time, I felt I knew what it meant to be one with the world. After our performance, watching the other delegations' performances, I realized how vast and diverse the world is and developed a deep desire to learn more about it during our two-week journey together.

One of the students I met on our journey was a student from France who wrote me a letter to say he liked the way I prayed before every meal, and there was a Japanese student who continually tried to sit next to me on the bus. But Ms. Kim was watching us like a hawk, so, much to our disappointment, there was no possibility for any sort of romantic relationships. We observed several couples among the students from other countries during our stay in Israel, but Ms. Kim was there to keep us "safe" by not allowing men to sit next to us.

Thanks to the thoughtful consideration of President Kim Ok-gil, we had the opportunity to visit several European countries including Sweden, Denmark, France, the UK, and Italy on our way back from Israel. This was a particularly precious time for us as traveling abroad was not a common occurrence in those days. Additionally, President Kim had contacted the embassies in the countries we were visiting in advance. As a result, the ambassadors greeted us at the airport, invited us to their homes for a meal, and made our trip even more memorable. During our journey through Europe, I was able to experience firsthand the civic consciousness that was not prevalent in Korea at the time, which held great significance for me.

After returning to Korea, I was invited to speak about my trip to Israel at several university chapels, including the campus-wide chapel at Ewha Womans University. The main theme of my presentation was "Let's expand our horizons to the world!" My travels had taught me that we should not live as if Korea were a world unto itself. There was a world that was bigger than Korea, and Koreans could learn a lot from other countries. Preparing the presentation was a valuable opportunity to organize my thoughts and solidify my decision to study abroad. With my father's support, I started studying for the TOEFL and made a concrete plan. I can confidently say that my visit to Israel completely changed my worldview and laid the foundation for my life abroad, which continues to this day.

Writing my memoirs has been a valuable opportunity to reflect on my life. I've been able to look back at the many experiences that made me laugh and cry while running the Rose of Sharon Foundation, the Vancouver Korean-Canadian Association, and the Vancouver Korean-Canadian Scholarship Foundation, and contemplate their meaning. I am especially grateful for the people I worked with, as I could not have accomplished what I did without them. Together, we made history. Although at the time I was simply living day by day, upon summarizing my life events, I feel as though I gave it my all and was rewarded for my efforts. I also acknowledge that there have been many hardships and injustices, times when I had to fight back tears due to difficulties or unfairness. However, I am happy to realize that those challenges are in the past now and I can look back on them and smile.

As I reflect on my life as a pharmacist, I am filled with memories of pushing myself to work tirelessly. I never missed a day of work, even when I was coughing up blood, and I would work without breaks for eight hours when customers were waiting in line. My philosophy was that every customer's time was valuable, so I always strove to solve their issues as quickly as possible. I received a lot of positive feedback for my efficiency, but I sacrificed my health in the process. I still don't know what the right balance is for me. Will living a life of hard work keep me vibrant and strong, or will it lead me to an early grave? I can only hope that those who come after me can learn from my experiences and use them to create a better life for themselves.

As I documented the life of my family, I rediscovered precious memories from the past. I felt like I was on a treasure hunt as I recalled my childhood, the time spent with my relatives, my love story with my husband, and heartwarming memories of our children when they were young. I had forgotten about these cherished moments in the hustle and bustle of daily life, but now I am grateful to have them recorded. I hope that these records will provide strength for my children during tough times. They contain the fact that their mother loved them very much and was always praying for them to live a healthy and happy life. I must also acknowledge that my life was so rich because I was with my husband, Dr. Oh Kang-nam.

I believe that my life is not meant solely for me, but for giving and repaying favors. I aspire to be of benefit to all those who cross my path. To achieve this, I am committed to living each day as if it were the first day of the rest of my life, making every moment count. Although I am here today, I know that one day I will leave this world. Therefore, I strive to love my loved ones to the best of my abilities and leave a lasting impression on those I encounter. I hope people will remember me as someone who spread love to their neighbors, gave back to society, and tried to live justly in a society where justice is often lacking.

One of the things I would like to accomplish is to build a

Korean community center in Vancouver. I believe there should be a strong hub where Koreans can come together. Currently, the Korean community enjoys gathering and working together to help the next generation and people in need around the world. There is also a growing number of successful Koreans living in Canada. By leveraging these resources, we can make our community better and have a greater impact. I have been pursuing this vision since I became president of the Vancouver Korean Association. However, it can only be achieved by the collective efforts of many people, and if Korean Canadians work together with a shared vision, there is no limit to what is possible. I am seeking more partners to join me in realizing the dream of a Korean community center. If it is God's will, I believe it will soon come to fruition.

I would like to use this space to ask for forgiveness from anyone whom I may have unintentionally hurt or offended. Although I hold dear the people around me, I humbly acknowledge my fallibility and the mistakes I have made. I ask for your understanding, and I will strive to live the rest of my life sharing that grace.

I'd like to thank the many people who have shaped me into who I am today. First and foremost, I thank my parents in heaven. My mother and father loved and devoted themselves to me from the time I was born. My mother, especially, moved to Vancouver at the age of 70 and cared for our household even when she was not feeling well. Thank you.

Next, I thank my husband, Professor Oh Kang-nam. Having

you as my supportive companion, my moral support, and my humorous entertainer in life is the reason why I am the person I am today and why our family is so happy. Thank you.

I would also like to express my love and gratitude to my three beloved sons, Eugene, Dennis, and Jason. Thank you for growing up so wonderfully despite the many moves and changes during your childhood. I would also like to extend my appreciation to my two daughters-in-law, Joanna and Bonnie, who have helped raise a wonderful and happy family with them, as well as to my four grandchildren, Nathan, Thomas, Owen, and James, who are all growing up well and thriving. I love you all and thank you writing your touching words.

There are so many other people I'd like to thank. First of all, I would like to thank my relatives and friends who played with me as a child, and my friends, teachers, and professors who inspired me to reach for my dreams during my middle school, high school, and university years. From the time I stepped foot on this strange land called Canada to when I moved to Vancouver and started running a pharmacy, to volunteering with the Vancouver Korean Association, the Vancouver Korean-Canadian Scholarship Foundation, and the Rose of Sharon Foundation, I have been supported by so many people. I hope you will understand that I cannot list everybody by name, but I would like to take this opportunity to express my heartfelt gratitude to all.

Finally, I would like to express my profound gratitude to the two individuals who made it possible for this memoir to see the light of day. I want to begin by thanking Professor Bong Hyeon-cheol for initially proposing that the recollections of an ordinary person could have value and for overseeing and guiding the entire process. Secondly, I would like to express my gratitude to Dongyeon Publishing House president Kim Young-ho for his hard work in turning the manuscript into a book.

I pray with all my heart that God will bless all who read this.

Oh Yoo-Soon Eunice, May 2023

Chronology

December 23, 1946	Born in Seoul, South Korea
February 1959	Graduated from Jaedong Elementary School in Seoul
February 1962	Graduated from Kyunggi Girls' Middle School
February 1965	February 1965 Graduated from Kyunggi Girls' High School
May 1968	Represented Ewha Womans University at the World University Festival in Israel
February 1969	Bachelor of Pharmacy, Ewha Womans University College of Pharmacy
March 1969	Served as vice president of Ewha Womans University Graduate Student Association
May 10, 1970	Married Oh Kang-nam
February 1971	Master of Pharmacy, Ewha Womans University College of Pharmacy
February 2, 1971	Immigrated to Canada
August 1, 1971	Gave birth to first son, Eugene
February 27, 1974	Gave birth to second son, Dennis
1975~1976	Attended the University of Toronto Faculty of Pharmacy
1976	June 1976 Obtained Ontario pharmacist's license and started working as a pharmacist at Park Central Pharmacy in Scarborough, Ontario
1977	Moved to Winnipeg and obtained Manitoba pharmacist's license
1978	Moved to Edmonton and obtained Alberta pharmacist's license
1978~1982	Worked as pharmacist at Owl Drug Mart in Edmonton
June 12, 1980	Gave birth to third son, Jason
1982	Moved to Regina and obtained Saskatchewan pharmacist's license

1982~1991	Worked as pharmacist and manager at Pinder's Drugs
1989~1990	Taught at Korean school
1991	Moved to Vancouver and obtained British Columbia pharmacist's license
1992~2014	Owned and operated Eagle Ridge Drugs
2000~2001	Served as director, Vancouver Korean-Canadian Scholarship Foundation
2002~2008	Served as chair, Vancouver Korean-Canadian Scholarship Foundation
June 22, 2002	Held charity concert with Jo Young-nam to raise funds for Vancouver Korean-Canadian Scholarship Foundation
2002	Visited Cuba
November 2002	Article featuring Oh Yoo-soon appeared in JoongAng Ilbo
2003	Served as president, Kyunggi Girls' High School Alumnae Association, Vancouver branch
2003~2005	Served as member of editorial advisory board, Vancouver Korea Media Newspaper
2003~2011	Served as first vice president, Advisory Committee for the Peaceful Unification Advisory Council, Vancouver Chapter
2004	Awarded Prime Minister of Republic of Korea Citation for social service
2004~2008	Consultant, Q&A on pharmaceutical and health-related matters, Vancouver Chosun Daily Press
2005~2011	Served as chair, Women's Committee, The Peaceful Unification Advisory Council, Vancouver Chapter
2006~2015	Served on the board of directors, First Steps, an organization committed to preventing child malnutrition in North Korea
December 2007	Gwanak Award, The Seoul National University Alumni Association in Vancouver
2009~present	Served as chair, Rose of Sharon Foundation
2009~2010	Served as president, Rose of Sharon Care Society
2009~2012	Served as president, Vancouver Korean Association
2010~present	Owned and operated Oh Pharmacy

2010	Received Awards for Excellence in Community Service from the President of the Republic of Korea
2010	Held Love Blood Donation Campaign with the Vancouver Korean Association
2010	Traveled to Brazil, Argentina, and Peru
January 2010	Held gilnori hanmadang with the Vancouver Korean Association
February 2010	Cheered for the Korean team at the Vancouver Olympic Games
April 2010	Held concert with Yoon Hyung-joo and Kim Se-wan to raise funds for Korean community center
August 14, 2010	Hosted Welcome to Vancouver by the Navy's Cruise Training Fleet event
September 2010	Held food tasting event with the Vancouver Korean Association
October 28, 2010	Held Fall Family Health 10K Run and Walkathon with Olympic Silver Medalist Marathon Runner Lee Bong-ju as president of the Vancouver Korean Association
2011	Received plaque of appreciation from the Korean War Veterans in Vancouver
2011~2012	Served as president, Ewha Womans University Alumnae Association of North America, Vancouver Chapter
February 19, 2011	Held Year of the Rabbit First Full Moon Festival as president of the Vancouver Korean Association
May 17, 2011	Held Family Walkathon with Other Ethnicities with the Vancouver Korean Association
October 2011	Received YoungMae Medal from Kyunggi Girls' High School
2012	Served as president, Ewha Womans University Alumnae Association of North America
February 4, 2012	Held Year of the Black Dragon First Full Moon Festival as president of the Vancouver Korean Association
May 2012	Held Korean business expo with the Vancouver Korean Association
November 1~4, 2012	Held AGM and annual festival for the Ewha Womans University Alumnae Association of North America in Vancouver as president of the Ewha Womans University Alumnae Association of North America
December 2012	Received plaque of appreciation from the Korean War Veterans Association of the Republic of Korea
2012~2014	Served as a member of the Multicultural Advisory Council, British Columbia

2013	Served as chair, Ewha Womans University Alumnae Association of North America
January 2013	Awarded Queen Elizabeth II Diamond Jubilee Medal from the Government of Canada
February 11~20, 2013	Nepal walking tour, Katmandu, Pokhara, and Sagarmatha
May 2013	Recognized by the Korean Veterans Association with plaque for community service
2014~2018	Served as chair, Vancouver Korean-Canadian Scholarship Foundation
July 2017	Awarded Senate of Canada 150th Anniversary Medal
October 29, 2017	Donated $1 million to New Vista Nursing Home Building Fund, also spearheaded MOU between Mugunghwa Foundation and New Vista, whereby the foundation pledged $50,000 per year for ten years
April 16~May 4, 2018	Walked the Camino de Santiago, Spain, and traveled to London and Portugal
May 1~20, 2019	Traveled to Da Nang, Vietnam, and Qingdao, China
January 2020	Recognized as a World New Intellectual by the New Intellectuals Association
October 2020	New Vista Care Home completed
March 2022	Housing development to be named Eunice Oh Residence
May 5, 2022	Selected to be a winner of the APOthecary Hero Contest by Apotex in recognition of outstanding contributions as a pharmacy professional in Canada
April 2023	Received thank you plaque from the Ewha Womans University Pharmacy Alumnae Association

APOTEX
Innovating for
patient affordability

May 5, 2022

Eunice Oh – BC
Oh Pharmacy Ltd.
504 Cottonwood Ave
Coquitlam, BC V3J 2R5

Dear Eunice:

Congratulations on winning our first APOthecary Heroes Contest – recognizing outstanding contributions of pharmacy professionals in Canada – in the Province of B.C.

We know the past few years have been a challenging time for our partners in front-line healthcare, but in the face of this adversity, it's clear you have gone above and beyond in service of patients.

As a small gesture of our appreciation, we will be making a $2,500 donation to a charity of your choice that aligns with the Apotex Giving Philosophy which can be found here. Your sales representative will be in touch with you directly to discuss this further. We will also be sponsoring an article in Pharmacy Practice to share the news about all our award winners.

For close to 50 years, Apotex has partnered with the pharmacy community and demonstrated our commitment to its success through multiple initiatives, donations, services and resources. This contest is one more way for us to reinforce our commitment.

Thank you again for your partnership and for everything you do.

Sincerely,

Jeff Watson
President & CEO

The Memoirs of Eunice Oh
A Life Story of Being My True Self

2023년 8월 21일 처음 펴냄

지은이 | 오유순
펴낸이 | 김영호
펴낸곳 | 도서출판 동연
등 록 | 제1-1383호(1992년 6월 12일)
주 소 | 서울시 마포구 월드컵로 163-3
전 화 | 02-335-2630
팩 스 | 02-335-2640
이메일 | yh4321@gmail.com
S N S | instagram.com/dongyeon_press

ISBN 978-89-6447-927-8 03040